TERRARIUM

TERRARIUM

33 GLASS GARDENS TO MAKE YOUR OWN

ANNA BAUER AND NOAM LEVY

Photographs by Rebecca Genet

CHRONICLE BOOKS

SAN FRANCISCO

CONTENTS

INTRODUCTION

"...Yon lindens for a seat I crave.
The few trees not mine own they spoil me
The lordship of the world I have."
　　　—Goethe, *Faust*, Part II

Two hundred years ago, Goethe expressed the irrepressible longing to keep a piece of nature at home. The sweet scent of the coastal scrublands at the end of a summer day or as the rain subsides; the unceasing singing of birds and insects in the mountains in spring; the delicacy of a cushion of moss or the texture of ancient bark: so many things remind us that nature has spoken to all of our senses for millennia.

Yet our cities were established by pushing nature to the periphery; since their creation, we have never stopped wanting to tame nature and reintegrate it where we live—with more or less success.

From this same desire and compelled by the same obsession as Faust's, we have brought the attempt to reintegrate green spaces to a new level: our apartments. As children of the city, we have tried to create landscapes that recall that lost love—nature—with the idea of growing plants inside often inert interiors. These simple designs, thrifty with time and water, have the advantage of being adapted to life in the city in needing very little care.

In this book, we describe the natural processes that govern these miniature worlds, and we offer many recipes to make your own terrarium, along with a selection of suitable plants.

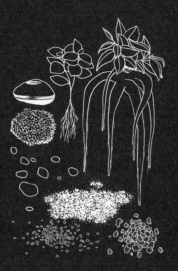

CHAPTER 1

THE ESSENTIALS

A first encounter with a terrarium often evokes the same feelings in viewers. For many, it is a way to absorb a distillation of nature from a sprig of greenery. We love to watch this little garden under glass, to see its plants grow and bloom. These miniature worlds function quite simply, on the same basic principles that govern life on Earth. With a few fundamentals of botany, you will understand, create, and sustain your terrarium.

WHAT IS A TERRARIUM?

A LITTLE ECOSYSTEM

A terrarium is composed of elements from the plant and mineral worlds, and microorganisms. We bring these together in a glass container to re-create a landscape. The container that shelters them becomes the place where they play their biological roles; they interact and thrive, players in a real ecosystem. A group of living beings in a biological environment is indeed an ecosystem. A closed terrarium creates an environment resembling that of a tropical rain forest in the guise of an artificial micro-ecosystem, with an almost self-sufficient cycle. The transparent, enclosing nature of the glass—in the case of closed terrariums—allows this self-sufficiency. The transparent glass lets in the light essential to the life of plants, and the condition of being sealed keeps the humidity emitted by the plants in the jar so that there is nearly no need to add water. As long as this landscape under glass receives a good initial dose of all the necessary elements to thrive (water, light, nutrients), it can live in near-autonomy for a long time. Human intervention can be minimal or unnecessary.

A different technique from the closed design is the open terrarium, which also assembles plants to create a small landscape, but in a container without a cover. This design method does not engage the same biological process: since it does not maintain its humidity level, the terrarium is not a self-sustaining ecosystem.

In keeping with the idea of natural designs without many needs, we choose plants from arid environments for this type of landscape. Cacti and succulents allow for easy care since they consume very little water.

NATURE IN MINIATURE

We make a terrarium the way a landscape gardener designs a garden, but in miniature. The art of the composition balances aesthetic and biological interest—true to the reality of nature.

Biology of the Terrarium

The choice of associations between living and mineral elements can lead to a beneficial symbiosis—or to a failure that will make you think you don't have a green thumb. Consider first the requirements of the plants in their natural environment before assembling the terrarium. The combination of plants according to their habitat needs—moisture, light, soil type—is accomplished by mingling plants that will not compete with each other at the level of their branches or their roots. If, for example, we don't combine forest mosses with cacti in the same design, it's because they don't have the same moisture requirements. The moss needs ample moisture to stay green, an amount that would spoil a cactus.

Aesthetics of the Design

Many of our terrariums are created according to our "classic" style: a central miniature tree that enhances the effect of a landscape in a jar and gives it its scale, with a few companion plants or mineral embellishments that recall the diversity at the foot of this tree in its natural environment. A rain forest tree, for example, such as a ficus, has beside it a luxuriant and colorful tropical plant such as a fittonia. Aralia, which loves acidic soils, goes well with ferns, which have the same needs in terms of soil type. Mosses are an important component of high-moisture designs; they may grow in flat mats (sheet moss) and evoke a tiny meadow, or some mosses grow in mounds (cushion moss) and create the impression of a verdant hill. Small stones become boulders; small dead branches or twigs are transformed into miniature mossy logs.

The Life in the Design

The goal, besides creating a small landscape, is also to let nature occupy this space: let the mosses and roots grow and the beneficial insects inhabit this miniature world. Sometimes when the terrarium is under construction, insects hide in the mosses or in the soil. Insofar as they are an integral part of the biotope, and if they are not destructive, it is preferable to let them play their role in the natural development of the terrarium (see page 26).

THE
ORIGINS
OF TERRARIUMS

History

It is difficult to identify the precise origin of the terrarium, but historic records allow us to trace back to one of its ancestors: the Wardian case. This was a hermetically sealed case made of wood and glass that could be transported over long distances, invented in the eighteenth century in the era of expeditions of explorers and naturalists. These containers permitted collection of insects and plants from their natural habitat to bring "new" species to Europe. The sealed design provides what the plants need to survive once removed from the ground: water and its natural cycling, light that can pass through the glass walls, and an even temperature, as if in a greenhouse. With this new way to convey living plant specimens, the botanical and horticultural world saw its collections grow and its geographic borders blur.

This invention brought to the West the tropical plants that we have in our homes and gardens today, and from this concept came the international pastime of plant cultivation under the glass of a terrarium.

The Inventor

Nathaniel Bagshaw Ward (1791–1868), a medical doctor, made the discovery when he placed the chrysalis of a moth in a bottle with damp soil. He closed the jar and a few days later found that ferns and small plants had sprouted and that condensation formed on the glass walls in the daytime, then trickled down onto the soil at night. A consistently humid environment was thus created. Ward collected numerous plant specimens on his expeditions to British colonies; his herbarium grew to more than 25,000 species.

HOW DOES IT WORK?

A living landscape in a jar is an invitation to dream, an object of curiosity. How do these plants breathe inside the closed glass environment? By what magic do they stay alive without being watered? It's necessary to describe the fundamentals of plant biology to understand how plants live and thrive, even under glass, and also why some designs will not work. One might think that this decorative display is inert, but it is home to living plants that need water, light, and a few other essential elements to live and flourish.

LIGHT AND PHOTOSYNTHESIS

Photosynthesis is the chemical phenomenon that allows plants and some bacteria, in the presence of light, to produce oxygen. It is this phenomenon that gives us, human beings, oxygen to breathe.

The Principle of Photosynthesis
- The water present in the soil is absorbed by the roots of the plant, and carbon dioxide in the atmosphere is absorbed by the leaves.
- With the energy in natural sunlight, these two elements, water and carbon dioxide, undergo a chemical reaction, called photosynthesis. This transformation occurs in the chlorophyll in the plant tissues.
- Light radiation breaks down and converts molecules into sugars necessary to the plant and oxygen (without which we could not live on Earth), which is released through the leaves during the day.

Photosynthesis in the Terrarium
Plants in a wet terrarium can flourish in the closed environment: they do not need ambient oxygen; they produce it. Be sure that your terrarium benefits from a good amount of light each day so that its plants can photosynthesize. There is no need to anthropomorphize in terms of trying to imagine how the plants feel—they aren't suffocating; they don't feel cramped. They adapt their growth to the available space, as in nature. In contrast, regular houseplants can live in lower light since they breathe the same air as you do (they do not need to produce their own oxygen).

SUMMARY

DAY
The plant converts water, carbon dioxide (CO_2), and light into sugars and oxygen.
water (H_2O) + carbon dioxide (CO_2) + light —> sugars + oxygen (O_2)

NIGHT
In the dark, photosynthesis pauses, but the plant continues to breathe. It absorbs oxygen in the atmosphere and releases carbon dioxide and water vapor.
oxygen (O_2) —> carbon dioxide (CO_2) + water vapor (H_2O)

oxygen (O_2)
water (H_2O)
carbon dioxide (CO_2)
sugars

DAY:
THE PLANT BREATHES AND PHOTOSYNTHESIZES

oxygen (O_2)
carbon dioxide (CO_2)
water vapor (H_2O)

NIGHT:
THE PLANT BREATHES, WITHOUT PHOTOSYNTHESIS

WATER AND CONDENSATION

One of the amazing things about a garden under glass is that, if it is well enough sealed, it can go without being watered. (Some of our terrariums have not needed to be watered for the past four years.) As with photosynthesis, the natural cycling of water is reproduced on a smaller scale in a closed terrarium.

The Water Cycle
Once the terrarium is completed, the plantings need to be watered. This initial supply of water is applied as mist or droplets on the soil.

This moisture is absorbed by the roots of the plants. Once photosynthesis begins, the foliage of the plants releases the water as a gas (water vapor) by means of the phenomenon of evapotranspiration.

This water then condenses as liquid on the glass wall. It trickles down to the soil, to be reabsorbed by the roots, and the cycle is perpetuated. Depending on the seal of the container, if the humidity inside becomes insufficient, additional water may be needed (see page 21).

What Kind of Water?
Besides simple hydration, water allows the transport of nutrients, minerals, and other elements essential to the plant. The type of water used in the terrarium is very important, all the more so because the amount is minimal and thus more concentrated (watering once or twice a year for a closed terrarium). Water with an excess of contaminants or chlorine can harm plants. It may be tempting to use tap water, but this is often hard water—with too much mineral content and substances harmful to plants, such as chlorine or nitrates.

Lime is also often present in water, and causes certain problems: it will weaken the soil acidity essential to many plants, and it will leave a white residue on the walls of the terrarium—and on foliage, which can eventually suffocate the plant.

The best water for the needs of plants is rainwater, which is very soft. Best of all is rainwater from the countryside rather than the city, where rain is subject to pollutants. If you live in a city, you can use a water filter pitcher or a reverse osmosis water filter.

———— water
– – – water vapor

THE WATER CYCLE

BUILDING THE TERRARIUM

In the design of a terrarium, every element has a purpose, besides being decorative. Along with the choice of plants, the soil type determines success: this is where the plant anchors itself with its roots, and where it absorbs nutrients and water.

Coarse Gravels and Volcanic Stone

We lay a bed of coarse gravel or volcanic stone at the bottom of the terrarium to help water drain from the soil, to avoid soaking it. Good drainage is essential for the plants, allowing the escape of any excess water: plant roots need to breathe, and they have a hard time if the soil is saturated with water. On a larger scale, in nature, this process is seen in the different geological layers of soil, down to the water table where rainwater accumulates. This is where trees send their deepest roots in search of water. In the same way, once the terrarium is developed, you will see the lengthening roots of the plants, visible through the glass walls, reaching toward the zones of greatest moisture.

Fine Gravels

The even layers of white, gray, or black gravel that we arrange above the drainage bed of stones in our designs imitate the sedimentary layers that can be seen on the face of a cliff. They too help disperse the flow of water.

Soil

The soil used in the terrarium must meet the needs of the plants that it will hold. Each soil type has its own identity in terms of chemistry, density, and nutrients. Some soil types support the growth of certain plants but would prevent other plants from thriving. In part this is why a cactus will not grow in a temperate forest. The volume of soil is small in a terrarium, so it is important to meet the plants' needs with the correct soil type, since it is neither effective nor desirable to keep adding fertilizer. To provide the best soil for terrarium plants, some commercial planting mixes do need to be enriched, which is why we often combine planting mediums.

Mosses

Forest moss, as a natural ground cover, helps maintain soil moisture. The moss slows evaporation, so it helps avoid excessive condensation on the walls of the glass container. Moss also plays an important role as an indicator of moisture level: if the moss is very green, the terrarium does not need to be watered.

Stones and Gravel

We arrange stones and gravel on the soil surface, between the mosses. It is onto this mineral layer that we add water to the terrarium.

Plants

All of the terrarium environment are assembled to help the plant—often a featured species and a companion plant—flourish.

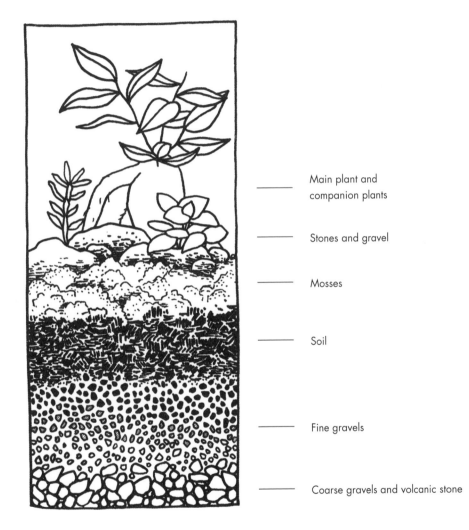

Main plant and
companion plants

Stones and gravel

Mosses

Soil

Fine gravels

Coarse gravels and volcanic stone

THE LAYERS IN A WET TERRARIUM (CLOSED)

TAKING CARE OF THE TERRARIUM

Although the terrarium only needs watering a few times a year, there are some problems to avoid so that it will thrive. The following pages give some tips for care. Generally you will only need to
- check the soil moisture
- prune occasionally to control the plants' size (you will not be changing the container when the plants' foliage starts to touch the walls)
- adjust the position of the terrarium according to ambient light in the room

EXPOSURE OF THE TERRARIUM
Less than 1 yd/1 m from a window
and without direct exposure to sunlight.

LIGHT

As we explained in terms of theory, light is the element that is essential to the process of photosynthesis; it is what allows the plants to breathe in the terrarium. Here is how to apply the basic rules to support the plants' vitality.

Exposure
Always set the terrarium close to a window but without direct exposure to the rays of the sun. Caution! At 1 yd/1 m from a window with northern exposure or lit from a light well, the plants will not receive sufficient light for growth and photosynthesis.

Even Light
Remember to turn the terrarium a half-turn every two weeks so that it receives even light.

Complementary Light
If you do not have adequate natural light, you can use a full-spectrum light bulb (6,200–6,500K) for 8 hours a day, placed at least 20 in/50 cm distant.

The Risks of Poor Lighting
When the light is not bright enough for a closed, wet terrarium, small, cloudy, whitish, mold-like filaments may appear—a fungal growth that must be removed as soon as possible to prevent further spread. It is an indication of insufficient light or excess humidity.

If you place the terrarium in direct sunlight, you may see black spots on the plants' foliage. The glass acts as a magnifying glass, and the sun's rays can burn the leaves.

WATERING A CLOSED TERRARIUM

In principle, a closed terrarium maintains the humid environment that allows the plants to cycle water. They live in near self-sufficiency, needing very little additional watering.

The Principle of Condensation
Like us, plants "perspire"—transpire; they produce moisture in the form of water vapor emitted from their pores, which in plants are called stomata. This water vapor humidifies the interior of the terrarium, allowing the plants to grow with the appropriate moisture level.

Some of the water vapor condenses, changing from a light fog to liquid again in contact with the glass wall. The water trickles down the glass to reach the plants. Condensation collects on the colder side of the container. For this reason the terrarium should be turned frequently so that this cycle happens evenly.

If you can't see the terrarium plants because of heavy moisture on the inside of the glass—whether from warm temperatures or too-direct sunlight—open the cover for about 10 minutes, enough time for the heat inside to subside and for the excess humidity to evaporate. This may mean that the terrarium needs to be kept better sheltered from direct sunlight.

If condensation on the glass bothers you aesthetically, open the jar for just the time needed to swipe the inside of the glass to make the moisture flow downward more quickly. But avoid opening the cover as soon as condensation appears, or you will disturb the self-sufficient cycle of the design.

Let the Soil Guide You
The soil will indicate the level of humidity in the terrarium. When it becomes dry at the base of the plants, it's time to water (usually only once a year).

How to Water?
Use soft water (low in calcium carbonate)—filtered water or rainwater. With a plant mister or by squeezing a fresh, wet sponge, water along the glass walls, at the foot of the plants, and over the surface gravel, avoiding the mosses. Depending on the size of the container, use from 3 tablespoons to 1¼ cups/50 to 300 ml of water.

WATERING ZONES

Care of Mosses
If you notice that the mosses are losing their green color, do not hesitate to take them out and dip them in filtered water, then squeeze them gently, like a sponge. They should soon regain their fresh color. Return them to the terrarium. Remember that the mosses' losing color is a sign that the terrarium itself needs more water.

WATERING AN OPEN TERRARIUM

Care for an open-style terrarium as you would for a potted plant, following the normal recommendations for the selected plants. The amount of irrigation needed, however, will be less because the substrate layer of gravel you place in the terrarium will help maintain the soil moisture.

In spring and summer, you will generally water once a week. In autumn and winter, the plants will rest, needing water only every two or three weeks. These are rough guidelines, not taking into account levels of humidity in your home. To verify the need to water the terrarium, check the condition of the soil under the surface layer of gravel. If it's dry, it's time to water.

TEMPERATURE

A terrarium is intended to be kept indoors. Outdoors, it could be subjected to fatal conditions, such as extreme temperatures or the intense direct rays of the sun.

The terrarium contains plants that need a warm, humid environment, so it must always be in a room where the temperature is 60°F to 81°F/ 15°C to 27°C. If the temperature goes higher, keep the container open and mist the interior to add moisture.

Don't place the terrarium close to a heat source, which could make its temperature too high and encourage mold growth or cause leaves to drop off.

BETWEEN 60°F TO 81°F/15°C TO 27°C:
LID CLOSED

ABOVE 81°F/27°C:
LID OPEN

PRUNING

Most terrarium plants are selected for relatively slow growth, the idea being to avoid a need to prune too often. You don't want to change to a larger container when the foliage touches the glass; instead simply trim the plants to keep the original proportions.

The Cut
When foliage presses against the walls of the container, either
- trim leaves (or)
- prune branches back, cutting just above a leaf node

In either case, leave the terrarium open for 24 hours so that plants can form good scar tissue.

Cuttings

PRUNING ZONE

Certain cut stems, especially those from succulents, can be propagated in the soil to start new plants. Propagation works well if softwood or semi-hardwood cuttings are taken in spring or summer, and hardwood cuttings in winter.

TROUBLESHOOTING

You Notice Molds Forming
From the first weeks, you may notice a fungus developing on mosses, branches, leaves, or stones. It generally appears as a cottony white or gray mold, when the different live elements in the terrarium are not yet acclimated. Remove molds as soon as possible with a clean cloth to slow their development until biological equilibrium is established. If mold grows on a large part of the plant, cut it to its base; if on a large area of leaf, cut the leaf off. Light will provide natural brakes to mold growth. It is important to follow the recommendations for light exposure to avoid conditions for mold (see page 20).

Black Spots Appear on Leaves
These can be caused by a fungus. Affected leaves must be removed to help prevent spread; then remove the cover of the terrarium for 24 hours to let the plants form scar tissue. Black spots may also appear if you have the terrarium in direct sunlight, which goes completely against guidelines. The sun, here more intense than the effect of a magnifying glass, will burn the plants, causing brown or black marks.

Foliage Turns Yellow
This can be a result of either too much or too little moisture inside the terrarium. If the soil layer at the foot of the main tree is muddy or waterlogged, or if the mosses are dark green and can be squeezed like a sponge, the terrarium was overwatered. In this case, the container must be left open for as long as it takes for the excess humidity to evaporate. Close it again when the layer under the surface is wet but not saturated. If instead the substrate feels dry to the touch, the yellowing leaves may result from the terrarium being open too often and/or they indicate that it needs water (a small amount; see page 21). The yellowing leaves may also

result from watering with calciferous water. It is important to irrigate with filtered water or rainwater, not tap water.

Green Leaves Fall Off

This is a natural phenomenon caused by the aging of the leaves or the need to replace them with young shoots, as in nature. If it happens frequently in the first weeks, the plant needs time to strengthen and develop its root system, and to adjust to the new humidity conditions inside the container.

Leaf Edges Are Dry and Curl in on Themselves

Leaves tend to dry at their tips or along their edges if heat is too extreme or humidity too low. If, passing your hand inside, you feel a significant change in temperature, the terrarium may have overheated and needs a chance to regulate itself. Leave it open for a few hours and then close it again. You will need to adjust its location in any case, when the seasons change, so that the sun's rays don't pass through the glass. If the soil feels too dry, follow the recommendations for watering (see page 21).

The Plant's Trunk Weakens

This usually happens along with the loss of leaves. The plant is suffering from overwatering that has decayed roots and base or may be victim to an organism such as one that feeds on wood.

Unfortunately, the latter is very difficult to get rid of, and you will probably need to change the plantings—and the soil if it has a moldy scent.

There Are Insects in the Terrarium

Not all insects are harmful in a terrarium. If you see earthworms in the soil, or centipedes, small snails, or small winged insects, you can let them live with the plants (unless you find them disturbing, in which case you can remove them). If you see slugs or large snails, remove them to keep them from eating the plants. They no doubt came in as larvae or eggs hidden in the moss from the start. You may also see small white cottony patches on or under leaves or branches: these are mealy bugs, which can be discouraged with biological pest control or insecticidal soap. Other potential pests are red spider mites or aphids. These are treated like the mealy bugs.

THE CONTAINER

WITH OR WITHOUT A COVER?

When we embark on creating a terrarium, several questions come up right away. The first concerns what plants you wish to include: some need a wet environment; others a dry one. The decision determines what type of container to use.

Wet Terrarium
Plants from a humid natural habitat (such as ficus, fittonia, and ferns) need high humidity to thrive. They belong in a closed terrarium (a glass jar with a glass lid or a lid of cork, plastic, metal). The cover must maintain the moisture level when closed, without being a hermetic seal. If the jar came with a plastic gasket, this can be removed. A transparent or translucent cover works best for even growth, permitting overhead light to reach the top of the plant.

Dry Terrarium
Plants from an arid habitat (cacti or succulents) need dry conditions. They belong in open terrarium designs, which do not maintain humidity.

LARGE OR SMALL?

The other thing to consider is the capacity of the container. The plants that you put inside need to be able to grow without requiring a trim every month. If your container is slim and tall, choose plants with a vertical growth pattern; if the terrarium is low and wide, select low or spreading plants. Avoid a bottle with a narrow opening if your plant is sizable and fragile, or you risk damaging the plant when you place it inside the terrarium.

WHERE TO FIND A CONTAINER?

Don't hesitate to reuse containers from a range of sources: a candy jar, apothecary jar, bowl, carboy, glass vase. You can find new terrarium jars in shops (see the list of sources on page 219). What is important is that the glass is uncolored and transparent so as to allow through the full spectrum of light, and so that the plants can achieve complete photosynthesis.

TOOLS

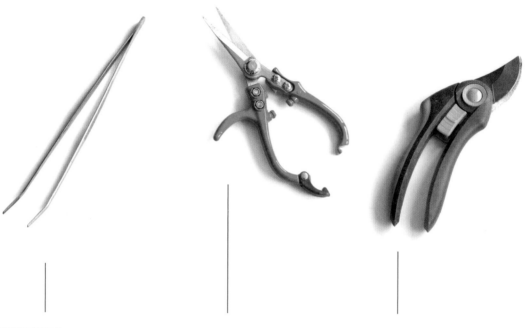

TWEEZERS

Long surgical tweezers
10 to 12 in/25 to 30 cm
long allow you to place
your plants with precision
inside the glass container,
especially in bottles with a
narrow opening, holding
the plant gently by its base.

SCISSORS

Small fine scissors are needed
to cut plants' branches or
leaves. Simply make sure
that they are clean.

PRUNING SHEARS

Use these for trimming thicker
branches and for bonsai.

MEASURING CUP

This is used to measure amounts of planting mixes and the gravels needed for drainage. You can substitute a 1¼ cups/300 ml mug for measuring.

PLANT MISTER

A plant mister is the most practical tool for watering in the terrarium. It allows for water to be distributed evenly and thus reach the roots. You can also use a fresh sponge: soak it in noncalciferous water (or filtered water) and then squeeze it to make a fine rain on the desired area.

FUNNEL

A funnel will help you put planting mix and gravel in narrow-mouthed containers. You can connect some tubing to help guide gravel along the edges of the container wall. For soils and coarse stone such as the volcanic stone for the bottom layer, standard funnels are too small; you can make one by rolling heavy paper or a paper plate into a cone.

CHAPTER 2

LIST OF PLANTS

Not all plants will survive in a wet terrarium (a container with a lid). The species that we have selected for the closed terrariums have been tested: we have verified that they can thrive in a closed, humid environment and that they will be about as happy as in their natural milieu.

In the plant list on the following pages, we give the scientific name for each plant, as this is the identification you can verify in a plant nursery.

KEY TO SYMBOLS

Light (distance of terrarium from the window):

☀ ☀ ☀ 3 ft/1 m maximum
☀ ☀ ☀ 20 in to 3 ft/50 cm to 1 m
☀ ☀ ☀ less than 20 in/less than 50 cm
The terrarium should never be exposed to direct sunlight.

Water:

🌢 ◌ ◌ once a year, only if the soil is dry
🌢 🌢 ◌ four times a year
🌢 🌢 🌢 once a month or more

Terrarium:

▢ closed terrarium (wet)
▢ open terrarium (dry)
▢ semi-open terrarium (terrarium is humid but opened occasionally)

A FEW DEFINITIONS

Here are some elementary definitions that describe characteristics of different plants. This will help you make choices about elements of the design.

Bonsai

The word *bonsai* comes from Japanese and means "plant in a pot." The ancient technique originated in China and developed in Japan until it became an art of its own there. The art of bonsai consists of cultivating a shrub while suppressing its growth, with the goal of creating a miniature tree. Techniques for trimming roots and binding twigs and branches give bonsai their gnarled shapes and their aspect of small-scale trees. Practically any tree species can be transformed to bonsai. They are the same trees that we find in nature but one sculpted and miniaturized by the human hand.

Deciduous

Foliage is not evergreen: leaves fall off for the winter, and new leaves grow in the spring.

Evergreen

Foliage is not subject to the seasons: there are leaves on the tree year-round.

Perennial

Temperate-zone plants whose roots or bulb overwinter, allowing the plant to fully grow again each spring.

Succulent

Succulents are also sometimes called "fat plants." Their name comes from the Latin *succulentus*, meaning "full of juice," evoking the thick, fleshy character of these plants. This physical trait permits the plants to store maximum water and nutrients so as to provide themselves with water over long periods; succulents easily survive this way in arid habitats. They are the result of a natural evolution whereby their leaves, which would otherwise lose too much water by evaporation, became spines or fat stems that lose less water from evaporation. The spines, for cacti, also play a defensive role.

LAWS

You can add to your selection for your terrarium with elements from your garden or from the woods. We remind you, however, to respect the natural environment around us. Gathering natural materials is regulated: know laws in effect in your area. Humans are unfortunately the main actors in the destruction of nature and cause the impoverishment of biodiversity day by day. In other words, make sure that in creating your terrarium you don't do it to the detriment of our planet. A small piece of dead branch, for instance, may be the home of larvae of an endangered insect, and if too many pebbles are gathered from a beach, it can accelerate coastal erosion.

FICUS

FICUS GINSENG

Scientific name: *Ficus microcarpa*
Origin: India, Sri Lanka, Australia,
New Caledonia
Description: Its trunk is formed by aerial
roots; *ginseng* means "root" in Chinese. The
young plant pictured here is not a bonsai.
Light: ☀ ☀ ☀
Water: 💧 💧 💧
Terrarium: 🔲

FICUS RETUSA

Scientific name: *Ficus retusa*
Origin: Malaysia, Borneo, Philippines
Description: one of the most
popular plants for bonsai
Light: ☀ ☀ ☀
Water: 💧 💧 💧
Terrarium: 🔲

FICUS PANDA

Scientific name: *Ficus americana*
Origin: tropical zones in the Americas
Description: a member of the ficus family,
which has around nine hundred species
Light: ☀ ☀ ☀
Water: 💧 💧 💧
Terrarium: 🗓

FICUS PUMILA

Scientific name: *Ficus pumila*
Origin: China, Japan, Vietnam
Description: a variety of climbing ficus, a vine
Light: ☀ ☀ ☀
Water: 💧 💧 💧
Terrarium: 🗓

JUNGLE PLANTS

SARRACENIA (PITCHER PLANT)

Scientific name: *Sarracenia*
Origin: North America
Description: carnivorous plant of cold temperate to semi-tropical habitats
Summer
Light: ☀ ☀ ☀
Water: 🌢 🌢 🌢
Terrarium: 🗔
Winter
Light: ☀ ☀ ☀
Water: 🌢 🌢 🌢
Terrarium: 🗔

AIR PLANT

Scientific name: *Tillandsia*
Origin: Warm areas of the Americas, north to North Carolina
Description: often grows as an epiphyte (without need for soil), able to grow on a branch, a rock, bark, telephone wire . . .
Light: ☀ ☀ ☀
Water: 🌢 🌢 🌢
Terrarium: 🗔

TONGUE OF FIRE

Scientific name: *Anthurium*
Origin: South America
Description: part of a large family of almost one thousand species, with widely varied flower forms
Light: ☀ ☀ ☀
Water: ● ◌ ◌
Terrarium: 🗍

SYNGONIUM

Scientific name: *Syngonium podophyllum*
Origin: tropical Americas
Description: one of the houseplants known as air-cleaning plants
Light: ☀ ☀ ☀
Water: ● ◌ ◌
Terrarium: 🗍

TROPICAL PLANTS

SAGERETIA

Scientific name: *Sageretia*
Origin: China
Description: known as "Poor Man's Tea,"
with foliage similar to the tea plant
Light: ☀ ☀ ☀
Water: 💧 💧 💧
Terrarium: 🗒

SERISSA

Scientific name: *Serissa japonica* (or *foetida*)
Origin: Southeast Asia
Description: The unpleasant scent
of its sap can attract insects
Light: ☀ ☀ ☀
Water: 💧 💧 💧
Terrarium: 🗒

POLYSCIAS BALFOURIANA

Scientific name: *Polyscias balfouriana*
Origin: India, Oceania
Description: Includes more than one
hundred species, distinguished by the
form and varied colors of their leaves.
Light: ☀ ☀ ☀
Water: 💧 💧 💧
Terrarium: 🗺

RADERMACHERA

Scientific name: *Radermachera*
Origin: India, China, Indonesia, Philippines
Description: There are about fifteen
species of this excellent houseplant.
Light: ☀ ☀ ☀
Water: 💧 💧 💧
Terrarium: 🗺

EQUATORIAL PLANTS

FITTONIA

Scientific name: *Fittonia albivenis*
Origin: South America (Colombia, Ecuador, Peru, Bolivia, northern Brazil)
Description: The many varieties of fittonia offer a range of foliage and colors (green, red, pink, orange, white).
Light: ☀ ☀ ☀
Water: 💧 💧 💧
Terrarium: ▨

DIZYGOTHECA

Scientific name: *Dizygotheca elegantissima*
Origin: Asia, Australia, Pacific Islands
Description: Unusual foliage ranges from dark green to black, marked with reddish veins.
Light: ☀ ☀ ☀
Water: 💧 💧 💧
Terrarium: ▨

MOUNTAIN PALM

Scientific name: *Chamaedorea*
Origin: Guatemala, Mexico
Description: A palm is often seen as an indoor plant. It was very popular in the Victorian era because it thrives in cool, dim rooms.
Light: ☀ ☀ ☀
Water: 💧 💧 💧
Terrarium: 🗐

GUYANA CHESTNUT

Scientific name: *Pachira aquatica*
Origin: South and Central America
Description: Its thick trunk allows it to store water and nutrients for long dry spells.
Light: ☀ ☀ ☀
Water: 💧 💧 💧
Terrarium: 🗐

HUMIDITY-LOVING PLANTS

ENGLISH IVY

Scientific name: *Hedera helix*
Origin: Europe, Asia Minor
Description: When the vine climbs
on trees and walls, it offers shelter to
numerous small animal species.
Light: ☀ ☼ ☼
Water: 🌢 ⬡ ⬡
Terrarium: ▣
* English ivy is considered invasive in some parts
of North America. A good substitute is *Heurchera
micrantha* (alumroot).

MUEHLENBECKIA

Scientific name: *Muehlenbeckia complexa*
Origin: Southern Hemisphere, Oceania, Americas
Description: Some varieties grow rapidly.
The full-grown form can reach 18 ft/6 m
and cover large surfaces.
Light: ☀ ☀ ☼
Water: 🌢 ⬡ ⬡
Terrarium: ▣

FALSE SIBERIAN ELM

Scientific name: *Zelkova carpinfolia*
Origin: Caucasus and Iran
Description: Many varieties of *Zelkova* are used for bonsai, most with deciduous foliage.
Light: ☀ ☀ ☀
Water: 💧 💧 💧
Terrarium: 🗷

PILEA (MONEY PLANT)

Scientific name: *Pilea peperomioides*
Origin: China
Description: endemic to Yunnan province in southwestern China
Light: ☀ ☼ ☼
Water: 💧 💧 💧
Terrarium: 🗷

FERNS AND HERBACEOUS PLANTS

RABBIT FOOT FERN

Scientific name: *Davallia*
Origin: Canary Islands, coastal environments
Description: This fern grows mainly
in broadleaf hardwood forests.
Light: ☀ ☀ ☀
Water: ● ◌ ◌
Terrarium: ▨

DRYOPTERIS

Scientific name: *Dryopteris*
Origin: Northern Hemisphere, coastal
and woodland environments
Description: Species of *Dryopteris* or wood
ferns grow in northern temperate forests.
Light: ☀ ☀ ☀
Water: ● ◌ ◌
Terrarium: ▨

ASPARAGUS FALCATUS

Scientific name: *Asparagus falcatus*
Origin: South Africa, Mozambique
Description: can grow to 21 ft/7 m in its native habitat; full size, because of its dense foliage, it is used as a hedge.
Light: ☀ ☼ ☼
Water: ◐ ○ ○
Terrarium: 🖾

OPHIOPOGON

Scientific name: *Ophiopogon*
Origin: Himalayas, Japan
Description: known for varieties with black foliage and blue berries. Its name comes from the Greek *ophis*, "serpent," and *pogon*, "beard."
Light: ☀ ☼ ☼
Water: ◐ ○ ○
Terrarium: 🖾

CONIFERS

BUDDHIST PINE

Scientific name: *Podocarpus*
Origin: Himalayas, Japan
Description: one of the oldest existing conifers.
Light: ☀ ☀ ☀
Water: ● ○ ○
Terrarium: 🔲

JAPANESE BLACK PINE

Scientific name: *Pinus thunbergii*
Origin: Japan and Korea
Description: emblematic among Japanese bonsai trees.
Light: ☀ ☀ ☀
Water: ● ● ●
Terrarium: 🔲

GOLDEN LARCH

Scientific name: *Pseudolarix amabilis*
Origin: China
Description: an Asian conifer that has the unusual characteristic of being deciduous. Its soft needles regrow each spring.
Light: ☀ ☀ ☀
Water: 💧 💧 💧
Terrarium: 🗐

CYPRESS

Scientific name: *Cupressus*
Origin: Mediterranean, North America
Description: in full-size form, traditionally planted in cemeteries in the Mediterranean region; also used as a windbreak in full form.
Light: ☀ ☀ ☀
Water: 💧 💧 💧
Terrarium: 🗐

MEDITERRANEAN PLANTS

OLIVE

Scientific name: *Olea europaea*
Origin: Mediterranean
Description: Some olive trees are more than two thousand years old!
Light: ☀ ☀ ☀
Water: 🌢 🌢 🌢
Terrarium: 🚫

THYME

Scientific name: *Thymus*
Origin: Mediterranean
Description: used principally as an essential oil and in Mediterranean cuisine; one of the traditional *herbes de Provence*.
Light: ☀ ☀ ☀
Water: 🌢 🌢 🌢
Terrarium: 🚫

MYRTLE

Scientific name: *Myrtus communis*
Origin: Mediterranean
Description: The leaves are esteemed in herbalism for their many benefits.
Light: ☀ ☀ ☀
Water: 💧 💧 💧
Terrarium: 🔲

TREE AEONIUM

Scientific name: *Aeonium arboreum "Schwartzkopf"*
Origin: Mediterranean
Description: a member of the large family of succulents. Found in areas of scant rainfall, notably regions of the Mediterranean.
Light: ☀ ☀ ☀
Water: 💧 💧 💧
Terrarium: 🔲

SUCCULENTS

EUPHORBIA

Scientific name: *Euphorbia pugniformis*
Origin: South Africa
Description: The *Euphorbia* family is a very large family of plants found on all continents except for Antarctica. Some species in hot climates resemble cactus, such as *Euphorbia pugniformis cristata*.
Light: ☀ ☀ ☀
Water: 💧 💧 💧
Terrarium: 🗓

SEDUM

Scientific name: *Sedum*
Origin: a plant adapted to every climate if the soil is well drained
Description: very widely distributed because of its hardiness and its drought tolerance.
Light: ☀ ☀ ☀
Water: 💧 💧 💧
Terrarium: 🗓

CRASSULA
"BUDDHA'S TEMPLE"

Scientific name: *Crassula pyramidalis*
Origin: southern Africa
Description: *Crassus* (Latin) indicates "fat,"
describing the plant's thick leaves that store water.
Light: ☀ ☀ ☀
Water: 💧 💧 💧
Terrarium: 🍃

CRASSULA FALSE
LYCOPODIOIDES

Scientific name: *Crassula pseudolycopodioides*
Origin: southern Africa
Description: This Crassula has the same characteristics
as *Crassula pyramidalis*, but its stems are finer.
Light: ☀ ☀ ☀
Water: 💧 💧 💧
Terrarium: 🍃

SUCCULENTS

PORTULACARIA

Scientific name: *Portulacaria afra*
Origin: South Africa, Swaziland
Description: in its native habitat, valued
as a forage plant by herdsmen.
Light: ☀ ☀ ☀
Water: 💧 💧 💧
Terrarium: 🍃

HAWORTHIA

Scientific name: *Haworthia fasciata*
Origin: southern Africa
Description: This succulent is in the same
family as aloe vera and the daylily.
Light: ☀ ☀ ☀
Water: 💧 💧 💧
Terrarium: 🍃

CACTI

BLUE PILOCEREUS
(BLUE TORCH CACTUS)

Scientific name: *Pilocereus azureus*
(*Pilosocereus azureus*)
Origin: South America (Brazil, Peru)
Description: a member of the large
family of candle cactus.
Light: ☀ ☀ ☀
Water: 💧 💧 💧
Terrarium: ▱

REBUTIA

Scientific name: *Rebutia*
Origin: South America (Bolivia, Argentina)
Description: abundant flowering. It produces
numerous shoots and reseeds easily in containers.
Light: ☀ ☀ ☀
Water: 💧 💧 💧
Terrarium: ▱

CHAPTER 3

LIST OF
MATERIALS

Besides the principal species and companion plants, the terrarium includes other elements of vegetation, as well as stones and mineral materials, decorative as well as constituents of the ecosystem. In re-creating a landscape, each element has meaning. Most materials can be found at nurseries and garden centers or craft stores.

RED VOLCANIC STONE
(POZZOLANA STONE)

Red-colored, porous volcanic rock, "red lava rock," "red pumice stone," or "pozzolana stone," it can be used as a soil substrate to drain excess water. May be substituted with other pumice stone, clay pebbles, or other small gravels.

Source: garden centers

CRUSHED GRAVELS

Ground-cover gravels of sandstone or granite, less than ⅜ inch/1 cm in diameter, often dark gray. Pieces have an angular, rough aspect. These gravels are often found in gardens, where they cover paths.

Source: garden centers
Where to gather: private garden

FINE GRAVELS

Very finely crushed gravel (less than ⅛ in/3 mm) improves drainage and is also used to cover the soil. It can be sprinkled along the edges of the terrarium to create the effect of natural geologic strata, or it can be used decoratively to cover the surface of the soil, between the mosses.

Source: garden centers

MEDIUM GRAVELS

Medium-fine crushed gravels (about ¼ in/6 mm) offer the same properties as fine gravels and create a variety of textures for the soils in the terrarium.

Source: garden centers

BEIGE PEBBLES

Decorative elements that enrich the landscape of plants with a mineral note, the warm tint of beige pebbles will highlight the sandy tones in a dry composition.

Source: garden centers
Where to gather: private garden

GRANITE
PEBBLES

Decorative highlights for the
surface layer of the terrarium,
placed between mosses in wet
terrariums. Dark pebbles change
color when watered, creating blue
striations. Some granite pebbles
are a lighter shade and rounder.

Source: garden centers
Where to gather: private garden

SMALL BLACK PEBBLES

Pebbles of black sandstone or anthracite (about ¾ to 1¼ in/2 to 3 cm diameter) can be used as a decorative layer to cover the soil.
Source: garden centers
Where to gather: private garden

SLATE

Rock from the family of schists, slate is used in terrariums for its appealing brittle texture and beautiful dark masses.

Source: garden centers, craft stores

FINE SAND

Makes soil mixes lighter.

RIVER SAND

Improves soil drainage.

CLAY

Makes soil texture thicker and heavier, allowing it to retain water more efficiently. Its pH is acidic.

SOILS

Plants vary in their requirements for soil types. Some need an acidic soil for their roots to grow, others need a base or neutral soil type. Soil mixes allow for substrates adapted to plants' needs. It's best to use more than one soil amendment, enriching the growing medium with a range of properties.

Source: garden centers

BLOND PEAT

Peat is slowly decomposed moss from bogs. It enhances the acidity of soil mixes.

ACIDIC PLANTING MIX/ ERICACEOUS COMPOST

An acidic substrate lightened with sand; poor in nutrients.

POTTING SOIL FOR INDOOR PLANTS

Enriched soil mixtures of neutral pH.

CUSHION MOSS

Widely distributed on poor, acidic
forest soils (oak or pine forests). In
a terrarium, a clump of moss can
evoke a little hill. The depth of its
green can indicate humidity level.
Source: florists, flower markets
Where to gather: private garden

HAIRCAP MOSS

Grows on forest soils that are poor in nutrients but rich in humus; shade-loving. It can grow tall; you may even want to trim it.

Source: florists, flower markets
Where to gather: private garden

ROCK MOSS

Widespread in shaded habitats,
on damp, noncalcareous rocks.
In a glass garden, the moss must
be hydrated frequently so that it
does not turn brown.
Source: florists, flower markets
Where to gather: private garden

SHEET MOSS

Common in forests on diverse sur-
faces, it adapts to bright habitats.
It must be moistened frequently,
without soaking it, to keep it green.
Source: florists, flower markets
Where to gather: private garden

LICHENS

A life form that is a symbiosis of
fungi and algae. Lichens thrive on
porous natural surfaces as long
as the environment is healthy and
unpolluted. They offer a multitude
of textures and colors.

Source: florists, flower markets
Where to gather: private garden

BARK

The textures of bark, varied according to species, make an interesting decorative accent. Be sure not to tear bark off of living trees—it's their skin.

Source: florists, flower markets
Where to gather: private garden

TWIGS

A twig from a tree branch found on the ground can be added to the terrarium to evoke a fallen tree in your miniature forest. Choose twigs already covered with moss or lichens.

Where to gather: forest or private garden

DRIFTWOOD

On the seashore or along the banks of a river, you can find pieces of wood sculpted and polished by the water.

Source: florists, flower markets, decorating shops

Where to gather: beaches or riverbanks

CHAPTER 4

TROPICAL LANDSCAPES

Tropical climates are characterized by elevated temperatures year-round (staying above 64°F/18°C) and by heavy rainfall. The climate allows plants adapted to high humidity to thrive, with many varieties of ficus and other species of plants with luxuriant foliage. The world re-created in the classic closed terrarium comes close to a tropical atmosphere. Ficus naturally becomes a key element in the design.

TAMAN NEGARA
FICUS AND FITTONIA

Ficus and fittonias come from a humid tropical climate. In this terrarium design, they evoke a dense jungle landscape, with a vigorous tree and colorful foliage inspired by the vegetation in Taman Negara Park in Malaysia.

CARE
Difficulty   🍂 🍂 🍃

Water   💧 💧 💧

Light   ☀ ☀ ☀

Container   🫙 🫙 🫙 | ▱

SUPPLIES
Glass jar (about 7 in/17 cm diameter, 10 in/25 cm high), with lid

Measuring cup

Plant mister or fresh sponge

Small scissors

DID YOU KNOW?
Ficus microcarpa is also called *Ficus ginseng*, which means "root" in Chinese, so-named because its trunk is formed by its upper roots.

INGREDIENTS
1 *Ficus microcarpa* (pot diameter: 2½ to 3½ in/6 to 9 cm)

1 *Fittonia* (pot diameter: 2½ in/6 cm)

1⅔ cups/400 ml red volcanic stone*

1¼ cups/300 ml planting mix (¾ cup/200 ml potting soil for indoor plants, ½ cup/100 ml river sand)*

3 handfuls of fine gravel, black and light gray*

3 handfuls of medium gravel, gray*

1 larger piece of granite*

3 medium-size clumps of forest moss*

⅝ cup/150 ml filtered water

*See the list of materials on pages 61–79.

1. Carefully clean the interior of the jar and the exterior. If necessary, trim the plants so that their foliage does not touch the wall of the jar. Soak the base of the plants in filtered water for 5 minutes so that the root ball is well moistened.

2. Gently pour an even layer of the red volcanic stone into the bottom of the jar. Be careful not to damage the glass.

3. Put half the fine black and gray gravels, and the gray medium gravel, in layers along the edge of the jar, pouring it along the wall.

4. Pour the planting mix over the volcanic stones and the gravels, making a bed about ¾ in/2 cm deep.

5 . Make two small wells in the soil deep enough for the roots of the plants. Gently loosen the roots. Place the plants in the wells and fill in the soil, pressing the plants in gently. Then tamp down the soil around them.

6 . Evenly water the soil at the base of the plants with filtered water, using a plant mister (or soak a sponge and gently squeeze it over the soil).

7 . Arrange the rest of the fine gray and black gravels at the foot of the plants.

8 . Place the mosses (damp, but not soaked) on the soil (not on the gravel, to not impede future watering). Set the piece of granite on the gravel.

9 . Close the jar after 48 hours. Take care of the terrarium following the advice on pages 20–27.

KHAO YAI PARK
SAGERETIA AND OPHIOPOGON

The national park at Khao Yai encompasses one of the largest forests in Asia.
The terrain varies from meadows to mountain peaks, with a rich diversity of flora
and fauna. Here grows Sageretia, also known as "Poor Man's Tea."

CARE
Difficulty
Water
Sun
Container

SUPPLIES
Glass jar (about 12 in/31 cm
   diameter, 18 in/46 cm high),
   with lid
Measuring cup
Plant mister or fresh sponge
Small scissors

CARE
For this type of design and because
of the fragility of the tree, open
the terrarium for a few hours on a
regular basis. Don't overwater; let
the soil surface dry.

INGREDIENTS
1 *Sageretia* (here, a 6-year-old bonsai)
1 *Ophiopogon*
4½ cups/1 L of red volcanic stone*
3¾ cup/900 ml planting mix (1¼ cups/300 ml of
   each potting soil for indoor plants, acidic planting
   mix/ericaceous compost, and river sand)*
2 handfuls of fine gravel, black *
2 handfuls of medium gravel, white*
2 handfuls of medium gravel, gray*
3 clumps of forest moss*
3 granite pebbles*
⅞ cup/200 ml rainwater or filtered water

*See the list of materials on pages 61–79.

STEP-BY-STEP

1. Carefully clean the interior and exterior of the jar. Soak the base of the plants in filtered water for 5 minutes so that the root ball is well moistened.

2. Gently pour an even layer of the red volcanic stone into the bottom of the jar. Be careful not to damage the glass.

3. Put half the fine black gravel along the edge of the jar, pouring it along the wall to make a layer. Make two more layers with the white gravel and the light gray gravel.

4. Pour the planting mix over the volcanic stones and the gravels, making a bed about 2 in/5 cm deep.

5. Make two small wells in the soil deep enough for the roots of the plants. Place the plants in the wells, pressing them in gently, and then press down the soil around them. The *Ophiopogon* can be divided in two; it is a plant that spreads.

6. Evenly water the soil at the base of the plants with filtered water, using a plant mister (or soak a sponge and gently squeeze it over the soil).

7. Place the mosses on the soil, letting them touch the glass, then lay the rest of the fine black gravel between the mosses, at the foot of the tree. Add the granite pebbles on top of the gravel.

8. Close the jar after 48 hours. Take care of the terrarium following the advice on pages 20–27.

KUNMING
PILEA

Pilea peperomioides, or Chinese Money Plant, is native to Yunnan province in southern China.
It became popular in Europe among gardeners of indoor plants before it was well studied by botanists.

CARE
Difficulty ♣ ♣ ♧
Water ● ◌ ◌
Light ☀ ☀ ☀
Container ▯ ▮ ▯ | ▣

SUPPLIES
Glass jar (about 7½ in/19 cm
    diameter, 13½ in/34 cm high),
    with lid
Measuring cup
Plant mister or fresh sponge
Small scissors

- -

AN ORIGINAL
The main difficulty of this design
is finding a *Pilea,* which remains
somewhat rare. You will need to
find a container wide enough for its
sprawling growth.

INGREDIENTS
1 *Pilea peperomioides*
1⅔ cups/400 ml red volcanic stone*
1⅔ cups/400 ml planting mix (1⅛ cups/270 ml
    potting soil for indoor plants, ½ cup/130 ml fine
    and coarse sand)*
2 handfuls of fine gravel, gray and white*
3 handfuls of crushed gravel, gray*
3 small black pebbles*
1 larger piece of granite*
5 medium clumps of forest moss*
⅝ cup/150 ml filtered water

*See the list of materials on pages 61–79.

1. Carefully clean the interior and exterior of the jar. If necessary, trim the *Pilea* to adjust it to the size of the jar (see page 25). Soak the base of the plant in filtered water for 5 minutes so that the root ball is well moistened.

2. Gently pour an even layer of the red volcanic stone into the bottom of the jar. Be careful not to damage the glass.

3. Arrange half the fine gravels in a layer around the inside edge of the glass.

4. Pour the planting mix evenly over the volcanic stones and the gravel.

5. Make a small well in the soil deep enough for the roots of the plant. Gently loosen the roots. Place the *Pilea* in the well, then gently press down the soil around it.

6. Water evenly at the foot of the plant with filtered water, using a plant mister (or soak a sponge and gently squeeze it over the soil).

7. Arrange the rest of the fine gravel at the foot of the plant. Place the damp moss on the bare soil, and arrange the pebbles and granite stone.

8. Close the jar after 48 hours. Take care of the terrarium following the advice on pages 20–27.

CHINA
YUELU
SERISSA FOETIDA

Another beautiful tree from the flora of China, from the forested district of Yuelu:
Serissa foetida. This is one of the rare flowering miniature trees suitable
for terrariums, with small, white, star-shaped flowers.

CARE

Difficulty ♠ ♠ ♡
Water ● ● ●
Light ☀ ☀ ☀
Container 🝆 🝆 🝆 | (◌)

SUPPLIES

Glass jar (about 9½ in/24 cm
diameter, 20½ in/52 cm high),
with lid
Measuring cup
Plant mister or fresh sponge
Small scissors

CARE

Serissa needs regular circulation of
fresh air to thrive in a jar. Open the
terrarium once a week for one hour,
twice a week in summer. Do not
water until the soil feels dry under
the gravel and moss.

INGREDIENTS

1 *Serissa foetida* (here, a 5-year-old bonsai)
3 cups/700 ml red volcanic stone*
2½ cups/600 ml planting mix (⅞ cup/200 ml of
each potting soil for indoor plants, acidic planting
mix/ericaceous compost, and river sand)*
2 handfuls of fine gravel, black*
4 handfuls of medium gravel, white*
2 handfuls of fine gravel, gray*
2 granite pebbles*
1 larger piece of polished sandstone*
3 medium clumps of forest moss*
⅝ cup/150 ml filtered water

*See the list of materials on pages 61–79.

STEP-BY-STEP

1 . Carefully clean the interior and exterior of the jar. Soak the base of the plant in filtered water for 5 minutes so that the root ball is well moistened.

2 . Gently pour an even layer of the red volcanic stone into the bottom of the jar. Be careful not to damage the glass.

3 . Arrange in layers the fine black gravel and half the medium white and fine gray gravels around the inside edge of the glass.

4 . Pour the planting mix evenly over the volcanic stones and the gravel, making a bed about 1¼ in/3 cm deep.

5 . Make a small well in the soil deep enough for the roots of the *Serissa*. Gently loosen the roots. Place the *Serissa* in the well, then gently press down the soil around it.

6 . Water evenly at the foot of the plant with filtered water, using a plant mister (or soak a sponge and gently squeeze it over the soil).

7 . Arrange the mosses flat on the soil, letting them touch the glass wall. Arrange the rest of the white gravel between the mosses, at the foot of the tree. Add the pebbles and sandstone.

8 . Close the jar after 72 hours. Take care of the terrarium following the advice on pages 20–27.

ANHUI

RADERMACHERA SINICA

Radermachera sinica is native to Anhui, a vast subtropical region in southeast China. This plant can become a tree in the right environment. It has a sweet scent when it flowers, reminiscent of jasmine.

CARE

Difficulty	🌿 🌿 🌿
Water	💧 💧 💧
Light	☀️ ☀️ ☀️
Container	🫙 🫙 🫙 ¦ 🖼️

SUPPLIES

Glass base and bell jar (about
  5¼ in/13 cm diameter,
  8¾ in/22 cm high).
Measuring cup
Plant mister or fresh sponge
Small scissors

THE CHOICE OF JAR

You can adapt a bell jar on any kind of base as long as the water that condenses on the walls of the glass can trickle into the base. Or you can use any terrarium jar with a lid.

INGREDIENTS

1 *Radermachera sinica* (pot diameter 2½ in/6 cm)
½ cup/100 ml red volcanic stone*
⅝ cup/150 ml potting soil for indoor plants*
1 handful of fine gravel, black*
1 handful of medium gravel, white*
4 small clumps of forest moss*
⅓ cup/75 ml filtered water

*See the list of materials on pages 61–79.

STEP-BY-STEP

1. Carefully clean the interior and exterior of the jar. If necessary, trim the *Radermachera* to fit the size of the bell jar (see page 25). Soak the base of the plant in filtered water for 5 minutes so that the root ball is well moistened.

2. Gently pour an even layer of the red volcanic stone into the bottom of the jar. Be careful not to damage the glass.

3. Arrange in layers the black and white gravels around the inside edge of the glass.

4. Pour the soil evenly over the volcanic stones and the gravel, making a bed about ¾ in/2 cm deep.

5 . Make a small well in the soil in the center of the terrarium, deep enough for the roots of the plant. Gently loosen the roots. Place the *Radermachera* in the well, then gently press down the soil around it.

6 . Water evenly at the foot of the plant with filtered water, using a plant mister (or soak a sponge and gently squeeze it over the soil).

7 . Arrange the mosses on the soil.

8 . Close the jar after 48 hours. Take care of the terrarium following the advice on pages 20–27.

SRI LANKA
SIGIRIYA
POLYSCIAS (ARALIA) AND FERN

With the heavy rains of the monsoon and a dry season, the island of Sri Lanka evolved luxuriant vegetation, of which ferns and *Polyscias* species are essential elements. Adapted to high humidity and heat, they can thrive in the closed environment of a terrarium.

CARE

Difficulty	🍂 🍂 🍃
Water	💧 💧 💧
Light	☀ ☀ ☀
Container	🫙 🫙 🫙 ǀ 🫙

SUPPLIES

Glass jar (about 7½ in/19 cm
   diameter, 17½ in/44 cm high),
   with lid
Measuring cup
Plant mister or fresh sponge
Small scissors

INGREDIENTS

1 *Polyscias balfouriana* (Balfour Aralia) (pot diameter
   2½ in/6 cm)
1 small fern (pot diameter 2½ in/6 cm)
1⅔ cups/400 ml red volcanic stone*
1⅔ cups/400 ml acidic planting mix/
   ericaceous compost*
2 handfuls of fine gravel, dark gray*
1 handful of medium gravel, light gray*
1 handful of medium gravel, white*
1 handful of coarse crushed gravel, gray*
2 thick pieces of tree bark*
3 clumps of forest moss*
⅓ cup/75 ml filtered water

*See the list of materials on pages 61–79.

102

STEP-BY-STEP

1. Carefully clean the interior and exterior of the jar. If necessary, trim the plants to fit the size of the jar (see page 25). Soak the bases of the plants in filtered water for 5 minutes so that the root balls are well moistened.

2. Gently pour an even layer of the red volcanic stone into the bottom of the jar. Be careful not to damage the glass.

3. Arrange in layers the fine dark gray and medium light gray gravels around the inside edge of the glass.

4. Pour the acidic planting mix evenly over the volcanic stones and the gravels, making a bed about 1¼ in/3 cm deep.

5 . Make two small wells in the soil, deep enough for the roots of the *Polyscias* and the fern. Gently loosen the roots. Place the *Polyscias* and the fern in the wells, then gently press down the soil around them.

6 . Water evenly at the foot of the plants with filtered water, using a plant mister (or soak a sponge and gently squeeze it over the soil).

7 . Arrange the mosses on the soil, letting them touch the glass. Add the gray coarse crushed gravel and the white gravel at the foot of the plants. Arrange the pieces of bark to evoke the forest.

8 . Close the jar after 48 hours. Take care of the terrarium following the advice on pages 20–27.

ANGKOR WAT
FICUS PUMILA, ANTHURIUM, DIZYGOTHECA

The site of Angkor Wat, one of the wettest places in Cambodia, is considered the heart of the country's biodiversity. These three rainforest plants live there.

CARE
Difficulty
Water
Light
Container

SUPPLIES
Glass jar (about 12 in/30 cm
   diameter, 12 in/30 cm high), with
   lid
Measuring cup
Plant mister or fresh sponge
Small scissors

VARIATION
You can substitute one of these plants with a fern but be sure to give it a more acidic soil at the fern's base.

INGREDIENTS
1 *Ficus pumila* (pot diameter 2½ in/6 cm)
1 *Anthurium* (pot diameter 2½ in/6 cm)
1 *Dizygotheca* (pot diameter 2½ in/6 cm)
3½ cups/800 ml red volcanic stone*
3 cups/700 ml planting mix (2 cups/450 ml potting
   soil for indoor plants, 1 cup/250 ml sand)*
3 handfuls of fine gravel, black*
1 medium gray granite pebble*
3 clumps of forest moss*
⅝ cup/150 ml filtered water

*See the list of materials on pages 61–79.

STEP-BY-STEP

1 . Carefully clean the interior and exterior of the jar. Soak the base of each plant in filtered water for 5 minutes so that the root ball is well moistened.

2 . Gently pour an even layer of the red volcanic stone into the bottom of the jar. Be careful not to damage the glass.

3 . Arrange half the fine black gravel in a layer around the inside edge of the glass.

4 . Pour the planting mix evenly over the volcanic stones and the gravel, making a bed about 1½ in/4 cm deep.

5 . Make a small well in the soil for each plant, deep enough for their roots. Gently loosen the roots. Place each plant in a well, the *Dizygotheca* in the center, then gently press down the soil around it.

6. Water evenly at the foot of the plants with filtered water, using a plant mister (or soak a sponge and gently squeeze it over the soil).

7. Arrange the rest of the fine black gravel on the soil at the foot of the plants. Set the granite pebble on the fine gravel and press it in gently. Cover the rest of the soil with the mosses, letting them touch the glass.

8. Close the jar after 48 hours. Take care of the terrarium following the advice on pages 20–27.

CAMBODIA
TA PROHM
FICUS RETUSA

The temple of Ta Prohm at Angkor in Cambodia dates from the twelfth century. The site has been kept with nature having the upper hand, to the point that the roots of the ficus trees are woven into the ruins of the temple.

CARE
Difficulty	🍂 🍂 ⬡
Water	💧 💧 💧
Sun	☀️ ☀️ ☀️
Container	🫙 🫙 🫙 ⎸ 🥡

SUPPLIES
Glass jar (about 10¼ in/26 cm diameter, 30 in/76 cm high), with lid
Measuring cup
Plant mister or fresh sponge
Small scissors

DID YOU KNOW?
This is a very popular ficus for bonsai. Easy to care for, it is quite hardy and adapts easily to life in a terrarium.

INGREDIENTS
1 *Ficus retusa* (here an 8-year-old bonsai)
1 red *Fittonia*
6½ cups/1.5 L red volcanic stone*
3¾ cup/900 ml planting mix (2½ cups/600 ml potting soil for indoor plants, 1¼ cups/300 ml river sand)*
5 handfuls of fine gravel, black*
3 pieces of slate*
1 piece of bark*
3 clumps of forest moss*
1¼ cups/300 ml filtered water

*See the list of materials on pages 61–79.

STEP-BY-STEP

1 . Carefully clean the interior and exterior of the jar. If necessary, trim the plants so that their foliage does not touch the wall of the jar. Soak the bases of the plants in filtered water for 5 minutes so that each root ball is well moistened.

2 . Gently pour an even layer of the red volcanic stone into the bottom of the jar. Be careful not to damage the glass.

3 . Pour a layer with half the fine black gravel along the edge inside the jar.

4 . Pour the planting mix evenly over the volcanic stones and the gravel, making a bed about 4 in/10 cm deep.

5 . Make two small wells in the soil deep enough for the roots of the plants. Gently loosen the roots. Place the *Ficus* in the center and the *Fittonia* to the side, then gently press down the soil around them.

6 . Water the soil evenly at the base of the plants with filtered water, using a plant mister (or soak a sponge and gently squeeze it over the soil).

7 . Lay the rest of the fine black gravel over the soil around the plants.

8 . Set the pieces of slate in the gravel, lightly pressing them in.

9 . Cover the rest of the soil with the mosses, letting them touch the glass.

10 . Close the jar after 48 hours. Take care of the terrarium following the advice on pages 20–27.

GUIANA
AMAZONIAN PARK
PACHIRA

The luxuriance of the rainforest in Guiana inspires this design. Guiana Amazonian Park hosts an important representative of the local flora, *Pachira aquatica*, also known as Guiana chestnut.

CARE

Difficulty	🍂 ♤ ♤
Water	● ◌ ◌
Light	☀ ☀ ☀
Container	🍾 🏺 🍶 ǀ 🏷

SUPPLIES

Glass jar (about 7 in/17 cm diameter, 14½/37 cm high), with lid
Measuring cup
Plant mister or fresh sponge
Small scissors

CHOOSING YOUR PACHIRA

Sometimes *Pachiras* are sold with a braided trunk. It's preferable to choose one with a single trunk, which is simpler and better adapted for growth in a terrarium.

INGREDIENTS

1 *Pachira aquatica* (pot diameter 2½ to 3½ in/6 to 9 cm)
1¼ cups/300 ml red volcanic stone*
⅞ cup/200 ml planting mix (½ cup/100 ml potting soil for indoor plants, 3½ tbsp/50 ml sand, 3½ tbsp/50 ml peat)*
1 handful of fine gravel, black*
1 handful of medium gravel, white*
1 handful of medium gravel, gray*
10 small black pebbles*
2 or 3 small clumps of forest moss*
⅓ cup/75 ml filtered water

*See the list of materials on pages 61–79.

1 . Carefully clean the interior and exterior of the jar. If necessary, trim the *Pachira* so that its foliage does not touch the wall of the jar (see page 25). Soak the base of the plant in filtered water for 5 minutes so that the root ball is well moistened.

2 . Gently pour an even layer of the red volcanic stone into the bottom of the jar. Be careful not to damage the glass.

3 . Pour half the fine black gravel, the medium white gravel, and the medium gray gravel in layers along the edge inside the jar.

4 . Pour the planting mix evenly over the volcanic stones and the gravels, making a bed about 1¼ in/3 cm deep, and make a small well in the center.

5 . Gently loosen the root ball of the *Pachira*. Place the plant in the well in the soil and gently press down the soil around it.

6 . Water the soil evenly at the base of the plant with filtered water, using a plant mister (or soak a sponge and gently squeeze it over the soil).

7 . Place the clumps of moss (damp, but not soaked) on the soil, and add the rest of the fine black gravel. Add the black pebbles on the gravel.

8 . Close the jar after 48 hours. Take care of the terrarium following the advice on pages 20–27.

TIKAL

CHAMAEDOREA, FITTONIA

The tropical forests surrounding Tikal were a cradle of Mayan civilization.
The fertile soil nourished the ceiba, sacred trees of the Maya.
This design includes other plants found in the jungle around Tikal.

CARE

Difficulty	◆ ♢ ♢
Water	● ○ ○
Light	☀ ☀ ☀
Container	🫙 🫙 🫙 ¦ 🍶

SUPPLIES

Glass jar (about 7 in/17 cm
  diameter, 17 in/43 cm high),
  with lid
Measuring cup
Plant mister or fresh sponge
Small scissors

INGREDIENTS

1 *Chamaedorea* (pot diameter 3½ in/9 cm)
1 colorful *Fittonia* (pot diameter 2½ in/6 cm)
1⅔ cups/400 ml red volcanic stone*
1⅔ cups/400 ml planting mix (1 cup/270 ml
  potting soil for indoor plants, ⅓ cup/65 ml clay,
  ⅓ cup/65 ml sand)*
2 handfuls of fine gravel, light gray and black*
4 small clumps of forest moss*
7 small white or gray granite pebbles*
⅓ cup/75 ml filtered water

*See the list of materials on pages 61–79.

1 . Carefully clean the interior and exterior of the jar. If necessary, trim the palm so that its fronds do not touch the wall of the jar (see page 25). Soak the base of each plant in filtered water for 5 minutes so that the root ball is well moistened.

2 . Gently pour an even layer of the red volcanic stone into the bottom of the jar. Be careful not to damage the glass.

3 . Arrange half of the fine gravels in layers along the edge inside the jar.

4 . Pour the planting mix evenly over the volcanic stones and the gravels, making a bed about 1½ in/4 cm deep.

5 . Make two small wells in the soil, deep enough for the plants' roots (give the palm a central spot so that its fronds can extend out). Gently loosen the roots and place the plants in the wells. Fill in the soil, pressing the plants in gently, then tamp down the soil around them.

6 . Water the soil evenly at the base of the plants with filtered water, using a plant mister (or soak a sponge and gently squeeze it over the soil).

7 . Place the mosses on the soil, letting them touch the glass (covering about half of the soil). Arrange the rest of the fine gravel and the pebbles between the mosses.

8 . Give the terrarium light and close the jar after 48 hours. Take care of the terrarium following the advice on pages 20–27.

ORINOCO

FICUS AMERICANA

The Orinoco River flows through dense tropical forests where more than thirty thousand plant species grow, with many species of ficus, including *Ficus americana*, native to South America.

CARE

Difficulty
Water
Light
Container

SUPPLIES

Glass jar (about 8¾ in/22 cm
  diameter, 13¾ in/35 cm high),
  with lid
Measuring cup
Plant mister or fresh sponge
Small scissors

INGREDIENTS

1 *Ficus americana* (here a 3-year-old bonsai)
2½ cups/600 ml red volcanic stone*
1⅔ cups/400 ml planting mix (about 1 cup/250 ml
  potting soil for indoor plants, ⅔ cup/150 ml sand)*
3 handfuls of fine gravel, dark gray*
2 handfuls of fine gravel, light gray*
2 granite pebbles*
4 medium-size clumps of forest moss*
⅝ cup/150 ml filtered water

*See the list of materials on pages 61–79.

1. Carefully clean the interior and exterior of the jar. If necessary, trim the bonsai *Ficus* so that its foliage does not touch the wall of the jar (see page 25). Soak the base of the plant in filtered water for 5 minutes so that the root ball is well moistened.

2. Gently pour an even layer of the red volcanic stone into the bottom of the jar. Be careful not to damage the glass.

3. Place a handful of the fine dark gray gravel and a handful of the fine light gray gravel in layers along the edge inside the jar.

4. Pour the planting mix evenly over the volcanic stones and the gravel.

5 . Make a small well in the soil where you want to place the *Ficus*, deep enough for its root ball. Gently loosen the roots. Place the *Ficus* in the well and fill in the soil, pressing the plant in gently, then tamp down the soil around it.

6 . Water the soil evenly at the base of the plant with filtered water, using a plant mister (or soak a sponge and gently squeeze it over the soil).

7 . Place the clumps of moss (damp, but not soaked) on the soil. Add the rest of the fine gravel at the foot of the plant and between the mosses. Add the granite pebbles on the gravel.

8 . Close the jar after 48 hours. Take care of the terrarium following the advice on pages 20–27.

RORAIMA

CARNIVOROUS PLANT

Mount Roraima is a fantastic place, a plateau isolated by cliffs 3,300 ft (1,000 m) high. Some of its flora and fauna are unique in the world. We have chosen the strange (North American) *Sarracenia* or pitcher plant to represent this place beyond time.

CARE

Difficulty	
Water	
Light	
Container	

SUPPLIES

Glass jar (about 8 in/20 cm diameter, 15¾ in/40 cm high), with lid
Measuring cup
Plant mister or fresh sponge

DID YOU KNOW?

Carnivorous plants evolved a unique trait in the plant world: they can capture insects, small frogs and toads, or small mammals and nourish themselves with the nitrogen from their prey's decomposition.

INGREDIENTS

1 *Sarracenia* (pot diameter about 5 in/12 cm)
1⅔ cups/400 ml red volcanic stone*
1¼ cups/300 ml planting mix (⅝ cup/150 ml of each acidic planting mix/ericaceous compost, and peat)*
4 small clumps of forest moss*
1 handful of small black pebbles*
⅝ cup/150 ml filtered water

*See the list of materials on pages 61–79.

STEP-BY-STEP

1 . Carefully clean the interior and exterior of the jar. Soak the base of the plant in filtered water for 5 minutes so that the root ball is well moistened.

2 . Gently pour an even layer of the red volcanic stone into the bottom of the jar. Be careful not to damage the glass.

3 . Pour the planting mix evenly over the volcanic stones, making a bed about 2½ in/6 cm deep.

4 . Make a small well in the soil deep enough for the root ball. Place the *Sarracenia* in the well and gently tamp down the soil around the plant.

5. Place the clumps of moss (damp, but not soaked) on the soil. Add the small black pebbles.

6. Water heavily with bottled water or filtered water, using a plant mister (or soak a sponge and gently squeeze it over the soil).

7. Keep in very bright light, but not in direct sunlight. Close the jar after 48 hours. Take care of the terrarium following the advice on pages 20–27.

CHIAPAS

SYNGONIUM PODOPHYLLUM

The tropical forests of Chiapas, in southern Mexico, are a vast, remote
region of dense vegetation. *Syngoniums* are abundant there.
They are also quite easy to find in garden centers.

CARE

Difficulty	◆	◇	◇
Water	●	○	○
Light	☀	☀	☀
Container	▮ ▯ ▯	▯	▣

SUPPLIES

Glass jar (about 5 in/12 cm
  diameter, 10 in/25 cm high),
  with lid
Measuring cup
Plant mister or fresh sponge

CONTAINER

To make this terrarium easier to
create, we used a simple food-
storage jar.

INGREDIENTS

1 *Syngonium podophyllum* (pot diameter 2½ in/6 cm)
⅞ cup/200 ml red volcanic stone*
1¼ cups/300 ml potting soil for indoor plants*
1 handful of medium gravel, white*
1 handful of crushed gravel, gray*
1 handful of river sand*
2 sandstone pebbles*
3 small clumps of forest moss*
⅓ cup/75 ml filtered water

*See the list of materials on pages 61–79.

STEP-BY-STEP

1. Carefully clean the interior and exterior of the jar. If necessary, trim the *Syngonium* so that its foliage does not touch the wall of the jar (see page 25). Soak the base of the plant in filtered water for 5 minutes so that the root ball is well moistened.

2. Gently pour an even layer of the red volcanic stone into the bottom of the jar. Be careful not to damage the glass.

3. Place the white medium gravel and the gray crushed gravel in layers along the edge inside the jar.

4. Pour the potting soil evenly over the volcanic stones and the gravel, making a bed about 1½ in/4 cm deep.

5 . Make a small well in the soil deep enough for the root ball. Gently loosen the roots. Place the *Syngonium* in the well and fill in the soil, pressing it in lightly, then tamp down the soil around the plant.

6 . Water the soil evenly at the base of the plant with filtered water, using a plant mister (or soak a sponge and gently squeeze it over the soil).

7 . Place the damp mosses on the soil, letting them touch the glass. Spread the river sand between the mosses and around the foot of the syngonium. Place the sandstone pebbles.

8 . Set the terrarium in a bright place and close the jar after 48 hours. Take care of the terrarium following the advice on pages 20–27.

MEXICO
SIERRA GORDA
TILLANDSIA

The valleys of the Sierra Gorda are home to exuberant vegetation. The humidity and precipitation support a population of plants that grow without soil, on the branches of the trees. The *Tillandsia* is among these epiphytic plants that have no need of substrate to grow.

CARE
Difficulty
Water
Light
Container

SUPPLIES
Glass belljar and base wider than the jar opening
Measuring cup
Plant mister or fresh sponge
Steel wire or twine; small scissors

CONTAINER
This design can be made with any glass container and a larger base to allow moisture to escape.

INGREDIENTS
1 large *Tillandsia*
4½ cups/1 L red volcanic stone*
3 small tree branches the height of the container*
⅓ cup/75 ml filtered water

*See the list of materials on pages 61–79.

STEP-BY-STEP

1 . Carefully clean the interior and exterior of the jar.

2 . Gently pour the red volcanic stone into the base of the cloche, making a bed deep enough to set the branches.

3 . Bind the branches together at one end with the wire or twine.

4 . Set the tied ends of the branches into the bed of volcanic stone so that they stand upright.

5 . Place the *Tillandsia* on the branches. Mist the base of the air plant, avoiding the foliage. *Tillandsia* does not like an excess of moisture.

6 . You can close the terrarium or leave it open. Take care of the terrarium following the advice on pages 20–27.

TROPICAL LANDSCAPES

MOZAMBIQUE
GORONGOSA
ASPARAGUS FALCATUS

Asparagus falcatus is native to southern Africa and recalls the expanse of the savanna of Gorongosa National Park in Mozambique. The plant's vigor will allow it to occupy all the space in the jar with its slender branches. The green moss represents the tall grasses on the vast plains in the rainy season.

CARE

Difficulty	🍂 🍂 🍂
Water	💧 💧 💧
Light	☀ ☀ ☀
Container	🍶 🍶 🍶 ∣ 🗒

SUPPLIES

Glass bottle (about 4½ in/11 cm
   diameter, 8 in/20 cm high),
   with lid
Measuring cup
Funnel and tubing (see page 33)
Long tweezers (see page 32)
Plant mister or fresh sponge
Small scissors

DID YOU KNOW?
This asparagus is used as an ornamental species, but it is related to the asparagus that we put on our plates.

INGREDIENTS

1 *Asparagus falcatus* (pot diameter 2½ in/6 cm)
⅞ cup/200 ml red volcanic stone*
⅝ cup/150 ml planting mix (½ cup/120 ml potting
   soil for indoor plants, ⅛ cup/30 ml sand)*
½ handful of fine gravel, gray*
½ handful of medium gravel, white*
5 small black pebbles*
3 small clumps of forest moss*
⅓ cup/75 ml filtered water

*See the list of materials on pages 61–79.

138

STEP-BY-STEP

1. Carefully clean the interior and exterior of the bottle. Soak the base of the plant in filtered water for 5 minutes so that the root ball is well moistened.

2. Gently pour an even layer of the red volcanic stone into the bottom of the bottle. Be careful not to damage the glass.

3. Connect the funnel to the piece of tubing. Guiding the tube along the inside of the glass wall, pour half the gray gravel and half the white gravel around the inside edge of the bottle, in layers.

4. Using the funnel, pour the planting mix over the volcanic stones and the gravels, making a bed about 1¼ in/3 cm deep.

5. Use the long tweezers to make a small well in the center, deep enough for the root ball.

6 . Gently loosen the roots. If necessary, cut 2 or 3 stalks to adjust the plant's size to the container (see page 25). Hold the base of the plant with the long tweezers and set the plant in the well, fill in the soil, and tamp down the soil around the plant.

7 . Water the base of the asparagus plant with filtered water, using a plant mister (or soak a sponge and gently squeeze it over the soil). Also water around the edge inside the glass to wash down any loose bits of soil.

8 . Place the clumps of moss (damp, but not soaked) on the soil, using the long tweezers. Add the rest of the gray and white gravel where the soil shows. Set the black pebbles between the mosses.

9 . Close the bottle after 72 hours. Take care of the terrarium following the advice on pages 20–27.

CHAPTER 5

TEMPERATE LANDSCAPES

A temperate climate is generally neither extremely cold nor extremely hot, but with a marked difference between winter and summer. Terrariums that are home to temperate zone plants (such as *Pseudolarix, Sageretia,* and *Serissa*) work best when they are left open at regular intervals to imitate the change of seasons—figure on a few hours open two or three times each week. The variable temperatures do not allow, in most temperate regions, for the kind of dense, lush forests found in the tropics, but they do support a high diversity of plant species, in particular conifers and deciduous trees, flowering grasslands, and perennial plants; mosses and lichens are of particularly rich diversity.

FONTAINEBLEAU

EUROPEAN FOREST PLANTS

With this design you can create a miniature version of the enchanting forest of Fontainebleau southeast of Paris. On a walk in the woods, you might gather in a responsible manner a selection of mosses, seedlings, and twigs from the ground, if local laws allow.

CARE

Difficulty	🍂 🍂 🍃
Water	💧 💧 💧
Light	☀ ☀ ☀
Container	🫙 🫙 🫙 ❘ 🍃

SUPPLIES

Glass jar (about 12 in/30 cm diameter, 12 in/30 cm high), without lid
Measuring cup
Plant mister or fresh sponge
Small garden shovel

RESPECT FOR NATURE

Gathering of plants or minerals from nature is subject to regulation. All of the living plants illustrated in this terrarium design were gathered from private property with permission of the owner.

INGREDIENTS

1 small fern plus a handful of the surrounding soil*
1 sprouted acorn plus a handful of the surrounding soil*
1 hazel seedling plus a handful of the surrounding soil*
1 sycamore maple seedling plus a handful of the surrounding soil*
3½ cups/800 ml red volcanic stone**
8½ cups/2 L planting mix (5½ cups/1.3 L acidic planting mix/ericaceous compost, 3 cups/700 ml clay)**
1 small clump of haircap moss (about 6 in/15 cm across)**
1 piece of bark from a tree stump, covered with moss**
1 piece of poplar bark gathered from the ground**
1 small branch gathered from the ground**
1¼ cups/300 ml filtered water

*To dig up seedlings, use a small shovel and keep as much soil as you can around the roots.
**See the list of materials on pages 61–79.

STEP-BY-STEP

1. Carefully clean the interior and exterior of the jar. If necessary, trim the plants to adjust them to the size of the jar (see page 25).

2. Gently pour an even layer of the red volcanic stone into the bottom of the jar. Be careful not to damage the glass.

3. Pour the planting mix evenly over the volcanic stones, making a bed about 2½ in/ 6 cm deep.

4. Make four small wells in the soil about 1½ in/4 cm deep where you wish to plant the seedlings. Place the fern, the sprouted acorn, the hazel, and the maple in the wells. Gently tamp down the soil around the plants.

5 . Arrange the clump of moss (damp, but not soaked), the mossy bark, the poplar bark, and the branch so that the composition resembles a forest floor.

6 . Water generously with filtered water, using a plant mister (or soak a sponge and gently squeeze it over the soil).

7 . Plants collected from a natural setting may hide insects or other small creatures (woodlice, ants, spiders . . .). Set the terrarium outside for a few days, protected from rain, so that they can escape. Then bring it inside and take care of it following the advice on pages 20–27.

CHAMBORD

FERN AND IVY

Ferns and ivy are typical plants of forests in France, companions to
the oaks and pines that cover the clay terrain of Chambord.

CARE

Difficulty	● ○ ○
Water	● ○ ○
Light	☀ ☀ ☀
Container	▯ ▮ ▯ ｜ ▱

SUPPLIES

Glass jar (about 12 in/30 cm
  diameter, 10 in/25 cm high),
  with lid
Measuring cup
Plant mister or fresh sponge
Small scissors

VARIATION

You can replace the fern with
another forest plant. If *Helix vedera*
is considered invasive where
you live, you can replace it with
Heuchera micrantha (alumroot) or
asparagus plant (see page 51).

INGREDIENTS

1 *Dryopteris* wood fern (pot diameter 3½ in/9 cm
  maximum)
1 *Hedera helix* ivy (pot diameter 2½ to 3½ in/6 to
  9 cm)
2½ cups/600 ml red volcanic stone*
2⅛ cups/500 ml planting mix (1½ cups/350 ml acidic
  planting mix/ericaceous compost, ⅝ cup/150 ml
  peat)*
2 handfuls of fine gravel, dark gray*
2 handfuls of fine gravel, white*
2 handfuls of medium gravel, light gray*
1 piece of tree bark*
3 gray or beige pebbles*
3 clumps of forest moss (diameter 4 in/10 cm)*
⅝ cup/150 ml filtered water

*See the list of materials on pages 61–79.

STEP-BY-STEP

1. Carefully clean the interior and exterior of the jar. If necessary, trim the plants to adjust them to the size of the jar (see page 25). Soak the base of the plants in filtered water for 5 minutes so that the root ball is well moistened.

2. Gently pour an even layer of the red volcanic stone into the bottom of the jar. Be careful not to damage the glass.

3. Put 1 handful each of the fine white and dark gray gravel and 1 handful of the medium light gray gravel along the inside edge of the jar, pouring them along the wall to make a layer.

4. Pour the planting mix evenly over the volcanic stones and gravels, making a bed about 1½ in/4 cm deep.

5 . Make a small well in the soil for each plant, deep enough for their roots. Gently loosen the plants' roots. Set each plant in a well and fill in the soil lightly, then gently tamp down the soil around the plants.

6 . Water the soil evenly with filtered water, using a plant mister (or soak a sponge and gently squeeze it over the soil).

7 . Place the rest of the gravels at the base of the plants. Arrange the mosses on the soil where there is no gravel. Set the pebbles on the fine gravels and add the piece of bark to evoke the forest.

8 . Close the jar after 48 hours. Take care of the terrarium following the advice on pages 20–27.

ASHDOWN FOREST
ENGLISH IVY

From the llama park, the original scenery of the adventures of Winnie the Pooh, or the royal hunting grounds, Ashdown Forest made a name for itself. Pines, oaks, and birch trees stud the heathland, and the English ivy flourishes.

CARE
Difficulty
Water
Light
Container

SUPPLIES
Glass bottle (about 4½ in/11 cm diameter, 8 in/20 cm high), with lid
Measuring cup
Funnel and tubing (see page 33)
Paper plate
Long tweezers (see page 32)
Plant mister or fresh sponge
Small scissors

VARIATION
Substitute an asparagus plant (see page 51) if ivy is considered invasive where you live.

INGREDIENTS
1 small *Hedera helix* English ivy (pot diameter 2½ in/6 cm)
⅝ cup/150 ml red volcanic stone*
⅝ cup/150 ml planting mix (3½ tbsp/50 ml regular planting mix, ½ cup/100 ml acidic planting mix/ericaceous compost)*
1 handful of fine gravel, white*
4 small gray or beige sandstone pebbles*
2 clumps of forest moss*
⅓ cup/75 ml filtered water

*See the list of materials on pages 61–79.

1. Carefully clean the interior and exterior of the jar. If necessary, trim the plant to adjust it to the size of the jar (see page 25). Soak the base of the plant in filtered water for 5 minutes so that the root ball is well moistened.

2. Gently pour an even layer of the red volcanic stone into the bottom of the jar (use a rolled paper plate if the jar neck is small). Be careful not to damage the glass.

3. Connect the funnel to the piece of tubing. Guiding the tube along the inside of the glass, pour half the gravel around the edge of the bottle. Pour the planting mix evenly over the volcanic stones and gravel, making a bed about ¾ in/ 2 cm deep.

4 . Make a small well in the soil in the center of the terrarium (using the long tweezers if the jar neck is narrow), deep enough for the root ball. Gently loosen the roots. Hold the base of the plant with the tweezers, set it in the well, and gently tamp down the soil around the plant.

5 . Place the rest of the fine gravel at the base of the plant. Let the mosses and the sandstone pebbles fall into the bottle and arrange them on the soil with the tweezers.

6 . Water the soil evenly with filtered water. If the bottle has a narrow neck, let the water run down the inside walls; this will also help keep the glass clean.

7 . Close the jar after 72 hours. Take care of the terrarium following the advice on pages 20–27.

VAL DI CORNIA

CYPRESS

The cypress, often seen in Mediterranean landscapes, is known for the fine scent of its resin. In the Val di Cornia in Tuscany, its elongated form draws the silhouette of a giant on the hills.

CARE

Difficulty	🌿 ♧ ♤
Water	💧 💧 💧
Light	☀ ☀ ☀
Container	🗃 🗋 🗋 | 🗑

SUPPLIES

Glass jar (about 5¼ in/13 cm diameter, 9½ in/24 cm high), with lid
Measuring cup
Plant mister or fresh sponge

CLOCHE OR JAR?

This design was made with a bell-jar with an opening in the top to permit the circulation of air. Cypress does not want constant humidity. If using a covered container, leave it open 3 hours each week.

INGREDIENTS

1 *Cupressus* Cypress (pot diameter 2½ in/6 cm)
⅝ cup/150 ml red volcanic stone*
⅝ cup/150 ml planting mix (3½ tbsp/50 ml of each potting soil for indoor plants, sand, and acidic planting mix/ericaceous compost)*
1 handful of fine gravel, dark gray*
1 handful of medium gravel, light gray and white*
3 small clumps of forest moss*
1 small gray granite pebble*
4 pieces of crushed gravel*
⅓ cup/75 ml filtered water

*See the list of materials on pages 61–79.

STEP-BY-STEP

1 . Carefully clean the interior and exterior of the jar. Soak the base of the plant in filtered water for 5 minutes so that the root ball is well moistened.

2 . Gently pour an even layer of the red volcanic stone into the bottom of the jar. If the base is glass, put half the gravels in layers around the inside edge. If the base is opaque, this step is not necessary.

3 . Pour the planting mix evenly over the volcanic stones and gravels, making a bed about 1¼ in/3 cm deep, then make a small well in the center deep enough for the roots of the plant.

4 . Gently loosen the roots of the plant and place it in the well, fill in the soil lightly, then gently tamp down the soil around the plant.

5 . Water the soil evenly at the base of the plant with filtered water, using a plant mister (or soak a sponge and gently squeeze it over the soil).

6 . Arrange the mosses on the soil, covering about two thirds of the soil. Set the rest (or all) of the fine gravels at the foot of the tree and between the mosses. Add the granite pebble and crushed gravel.

7 . Close the jar after 48 hours. Take care of the terrarium following the advice on pages 20–27.

THE BLACK FOREST

FERNS

This design is inspired by the Black Forest, in the west of Germany,
one of the most protected forest regions in the country.
Ferns and ivy represent a small piece of the landscape.

CARE

Difficulty	◆	◇	◇
Water	●	◌	◌
Light	☀	☀	☀
Container	▢	▢	▮ ∣ ▧

SUPPLIES

Glass jar (about 10½ in/26.5 cm
    diameter, 17½ in/44.5 cm high),
    with lid
Measuring cup
Plant mister or fresh sponge
Small scissors

VARIATION

You can replace the ivy with an
asparagus plant (page 51) if ivy is
considered invasive where you live.

INGREDIENTS

2 or 3 kinds of *Dryopteris* or *Asplenium* ferns,
    according to the size that you find
1 *Hedera helix* English ivy (pot diameter 2½ to
    3½ in/6 to 9 cm)
3½ cups/800 ml red volcanic stone*
6¼ cups/1.5 L planting mix (4¼ cups/1 L acidic
    planting mix/ericaceous compost, 2 cups/500 ml
    peat)*
1 handful of fine gravel, light gray*
1 handful of fine gravel, dark gray*
1 handful of fine gravel, white*
1 piece of slate*
5 slabs of forest moss*
1 thin tree branch (about ⅜ in/1 cm diameter,
    10 in/25 cm long)*
A few pieces of bark gathered from the ground*
⅞ cup/200 ml filtered water

*See the list of materials on pages 61–79.

STEP-BY-STEP

1. Carefully clean the interior and exterior of the jar. If necessary, trim the plants so that their foliage does not touch the wall of the jar (see page 25). Soak the base of the plants in filtered water for 5 minutes so that the root ball is well moistened.

2. Gently pour an even layer of the red volcanic stone into the bottom of the jar, keeping a few pieces to decorate the surface ground.

3. Arrange half the fine gravels around the inside edge of the jar. Pour the planting mix evenly over the volcanic stones and gravels.

4. Make small wells in the soil about 2 in/5 cm deep for the plants, spaced so the fronds of the ferns do not become tangled at first.

5. Gently loosen the roots of the plants and place them in the wells, fill in the soil lightly, then gently tamp down the soil around the plants.

6 . Sink the tree branch at the foot of the vine, down to the layer of volcanic stone to give the plant support.

7 . Arrange the mosses, covering about one third of the soil, the branch, and the pieces of bark to resemble the forest floor.

8 . Set the rest of the gravels between the mosses and at the foot of the plants. Place the piece of slate and the remaining volcanic stones on the light gravels.

9 . Water the soil evenly on the surface with filtered water, using a plant mister (or soak a sponge and gently squeeze it over the soil).

10 . Leave the terrarium in dim light for 48 hours. Take care of the terrarium following the advice on pages 20–27.

KAHURANGI

MUEHLENBECKIA

Muehlenbeckia is a spreading plant native to New Zealand that can live perfectly in a closed terrarium. The plant is found in particular in the park of Kahurangi, where it grows in dense stands among giant tree ferns.

CARE

Difficulty	● ◇ ◇
Water	● ◇ ◇
Light	☀ ☀ ☀
Container	▯ ▮ ▯ ׀ ▱

SUPPLIES

Glass jar (about 7½ in/19 cm diameter, 13½ in/34 cm high), with lid
Measuring cup
Plant mister or fresh sponge
Small scissors

IT GROWS

You can let the plant grow untamed or you can prune it from time to time to adapt it to the size of the jar (see page 25).

INGREDIENTS

1 *Muehlenbeckia complexa*
1⅔ cups/400 ml red volcanic stone*
1¼ cups/300 ml planting mix (⅝ cup/100 ml of each potting soil for indoor plants and fine and coarse sand)*
2 handfuls of fine gravel, dark gray*
4 handfuls of medium gravel, light gray*
2 handfuls of black stones*
1 or 2 pieces of granite*
4 or 5 clumps of forest moss*
⅝ cup/150 ml filtered water

*See the list of materials on pages 61–79.

1. Carefully clean the interior and exterior of the jar. If necessary, trim the plant to adjust it to the size of the jar (see page 25). Soak the base of the plant in filtered water for 5 minutes so that the root ball is well moistened.

2. Gently pour an even layer of the red volcanic stone into the bottom of the jar. Be careful not to damage the glass.

3. Arrange half the fine dark gray gravel and half the medium light gray gravel in layers around the inside edge of the jar.

4. Pour the planting mix evenly over the volcanic stones and gravels.

5 . Make a small well in the soil deep enough for the roots of the plant. Gently loosen the roots of the plant and place it in the wells, fill in the soil lightly, then gently tamp down the soil around the plant.

6 . Water the soil evenly at the foot of the plant with filtered water, using a plant mister (or soak a sponge and gently squeeze it over the soil).

7 . Arrange the rest of the fine and medium gravels at the foot of the plant and add the stones and granite. Place the mosses (damp, but not soaked), on the bare soil.

8 . Close the jar after 48 hours. Take care of the terrarium following the advice on pages 20–27.

OSHIMA ISLAND

JAPANESE BLACK PINE

Oshima Island provides the *Pinus thunbergii* Japanese black pine, chosen for this design, an ideal, moderate coastal climate, but the tree will adapt well to your glass garden if the humidity is kept constant and if given good light.

CARE

Difficulty	🍂 🍂 🍂
Water	💧 💧 💧
Light	☀ ☀ ☀
Container	🗋 🗋 🗋 ⏐ 🖼

SUPPLIES

Glass jar (about 10¼ in/26 cm diameter, 22 in/56 cm high), without lid
Measuring cup
Plant mister or fresh sponge
Small scissors

VARIATION

You can substitute the Japanese pine with a juniper.

WATERING

Water frequently, adjusting for the ambient humidity.

INGREDIENTS

1 *Pinus thunbergii* (Japanese black pine, here an 8-year-old bonsai)
4½ cups/1 L red volcanic stone
3¾ cup/900 ml acidic planting mix/ericaceous compost
3 handfuls of medium gravel, white*
3 handfuls of sandstone pebbles, black*
4 gray granite pebbles*
2 small dry branches*
2 pieces of rock moss*
1 piece of haircap moss*
1 cup/250 ml filtered water

*See the list of materials on pages 61–79.

1. Carefully clean the interior and exterior of the jar. Soak the base of the plant in filtered water for 5 minutes so that the root ball is well moistened.

2. Gently pour an even layer of the red volcanic stone into the bottom of the jar. Be careful not to damage the glass.

3. Arrange half of the gravel in a layer along the edge of the jar, pouring it along the wall.

4. Pour the acidic planting mix evenly over the volcanic stones and gravel, making a bed about 1¼ in/3 cm deep.

5 . Make a small well in the soil deep enough for the roots of the pine. Loosen the roots and place the pine in the well, fill in the soil lightly, then gently tamp down the soil around the plant.

6 . Water the soil evenly at the base of the plant with filtered water, using a plant mister (or soak a sponge and gently squeeze it over the soil).

7 . Arrange the mosses on the soil, letting them touch the glass.

8 . Arrange the rest of the gravel and the black sandstone pebbles between the mosses, at the foot of the tree. Add the gray granite pebbles and the dry branches. Take care of the terrarium following the advice on pages 20–27.

KYUSHU
PODOCARPUS AND OPHIOPOGON

This design brings together plants that evoke the island of Kyushu, such as this conifer, a subtropical pine, or the ophiopogon, a spreading plant with beautiful blue berries.

CARE

Difficulty
Water
Light
Container

SUPPLIES

Glass jar (about 10¼ in/26 cm diameter, 13¾ in/35 cm high), with lid
Measuring cup
Plant mister or fresh sponge
Small scissors

DID YOU KNOW?

Ophiopogon japonicus produces fruit of an intense blue, but it is inedible. You can substitute with a fern, adding a handful of peat around its roots.

INGREDIENTS

1 *Podocarpus* (here, a 4-year-old bonsai)
1 *Ophiopogon*
2½ cups/600 ml red volcanic stone*
2½ cups/600 ml planting mix (2 cups/450 ml potting soil for indoor plants, ½ cup/150 ml acidic planting mix/ericaceous compost)*
4 handfuls of fine gravel, dark gray*
3 handfuls of fine gravel, black*
2 handfuls of medium gravel, white*
2 granite pebbles*
4 medium clumps of forest moss*
⅝ cup/150 ml filtered water

*See the list of materials on pages 61–79.

1. Carefully clean the interior and exterior of the jar. Soak the base of the plants in filtered water for 5 minutes so that the root ball is well moistened.

2. Gently pour an even layer of the red volcanic stone into the bottom of the jar. Be careful not to damage the glass.

3. Arrange half the fine black gravel and all of the white and gray gravels in layers around the inside edge of the jar.

4. Pour the planting mix evenly over the volcanic stones and gravels, making a bed about 2 in/5 cm deep.

5 . Make two small wells in the soil where you want to put the bonsai and the *Ophiopogon*. Loosen the roots of the plants and place them in the wells, fill in the soil lightly, then gently tamp down the soil around the plants.

6 . Water the soil evenly at the foot of the plants with filtered water, using a plant mister (or soak a sponge and gently squeeze it over the soil).

7 . Place the damp mosses on the soil, letting them touch the glass. Lay the rest of the gravel between the mosses, at the foot of the plants. Add the pebbles.

8 . Close the jar after 48 hours. Take care of the terrarium following the advice on pages 20–27.

CHINA
MOUNT LUOFU
ZELKOVA

On this sacred Chinese mountain, Mount Luofu, the Siberian elm (*Zelkova*) grows in a wet, temperate climate.

CARE
Difficulty
Water
Light
Container

SUPPLIES
Glass jar (about 7½ in/19 cm diameter, 17½ in/44 cm high), with lid
Measuring cup
Plant mister or fresh sponge
Small scissors

CARE
For this type of design and because of the fragility of the tree, open the terrarium for a few hours often. Do not water unless the soil gets dry beneath the moss and gravel.

INGREDIENTS
1 *Zelkova carpinifolia* (here, a 4-year-old bonsai)
1⅔ cups/400 ml red volcanic stone*
1½ cups/390 ml planting mix (½ cup/130 ml of each potting soil for indoor plants, acidic planting mix/ericaceous compost, and river sand)*
2 handfuls of fine gravel, dark gray*
2 handfuls of fine gravel, white*
3 clumps of forest moss*
5 small black sandstone pebbles*
⅝ cup/150 ml filtered water

*See the list of materials on pages 61–79.

STEP-BY-STEP

1. Carefully clean the interior and exterior of the jar. Soak the base of the plant in filtered water for 5 minutes so that the root ball is well moistened.

2. Gently pour an even layer of the red volcanic stone into the bottom of the jar. Be careful not to damage the glass.

3. Pour half the gray and white gravels in layers around the inside edge of the jar.

4. Pour the planting mix evenly over the volcanic stones and gravels, making a bed about 2 in/5 cm deep.

5 . Make a well in the soil deep enough for the roots of the *Zelkova*. Gently loosen the roots. Place the plant in the well and fill in the soil, pressing the plant in gently, then tamp down the soil around it.

6 . Water the soil evenly on the surface with filtered water, using a plant mister (or soak a sponge and gently squeeze it over the soil).

7 . Place the damp mosses on the soil, letting them touch the glass. Lay the rest of the fine gravel between the mosses, at the foot of the tree. Add the black sandstone pebbles.

8 . Close the jar after 48 hours. Take care of the terrarium following the advice on pages 20–27.

CHINA

LAKE TAI

GOLDEN LARCH

The golden larch (or "false larch") is one of our favorites for larger designs.
This Chinese conifer appreciates humidity and a temperate climate. They thrive
around Lake Tai, where the blue waters reflect their graceful crowns.

CARE
Difficulty
Water
Light
Container

SUPPLIES
Glass jar (about 12½ in/32 cm
   diameter, 25½ in/65 cm high),
   with lid
Measuring cup
Plant mister or fresh sponge
Small scissors

AN OPEN TERRARIUM IN
SUMMER
In summer, it's good to leave this
terrarium completely open and
water accordingly, since this tree
suffers from high heat (over 77° F/
25° C).

INGREDIENTS
1 *Pseudolarix* golden larch (here, an 8-year-old
   bonsai)
3¾ cup/900 ml red volcanic stone*
6¾ cups/1.5 L planting mix (2¼ cups/500 ml of
   each acidic planting mix/ericaceous compost,
   potting soil for indoor plants, and clay)*
3 handfuls of medium gravel, white*
6 handfuls of fine gravel, gray*
3 handfuls of crushed gravel, gray*
1 handful of slate in small pieces*
4 large clumps of forest moss*
1 pine cone
1 tree branch*
1¼ cups/300 ml filtered water

*See the list of materials on pages 61–79.

1 . Carefully clean the interior and exterior of the jar. Soak the base of the tree in filtered water for 5 minutes so that the root ball is well moistened.

2 . Gently pour an even layer of the red volcanic stone into the bottom of the jar. Be careful not to damage the glass.

3 . Pour half the white gravel and half the gray gravel in layers around the inside edge of the jar.

4 . Pour the planting mix evenly over the volcanic stones and gravels, making a bed about 2¾ in/7 cm deep.

5 . Make a small well in the soil deep enough for the roots of the tree. Gently loosen the roots. Place the plant in the well and fill in the soil, pressing the plant in gently, then tamp down the soil around it.

6 . Water the soil evenly at the foot of the tree with filtered water, using a plant mister (or soak a sponge and gently squeeze it over the soil).

7 . Place the damp mosses on the soil, letting them touch the glass. Lay the rest of the gravels, the pieces of slate, and the crushed gravel between the mosses and at the foot of the tree. Add the pine cone and the branch to the arrangement.

8 . Close the jar after 72 hours; open the terrarium frequently. Take care of the terrarium following the advice on pages 20–27.

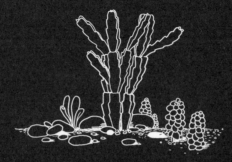

CHAPTER 6

ARID LANDSCAPES

Many geographic zones in the world have an arid climate, from deserts to high plateaus. These regions see high temperatures in summer and drought conditions that considerably restrict development of plants and animals. This is the country of succulents and cacti, plants that can store water from rare wet periods to nourish themselves from these reserves during the rest of the year. In a terrarium, these plants must be rarely watered, least of all in winter, which corresponds to their natural dry season. The low density of vegetation in these parts of the world trades for the beauty of the mineral kingdom. It is pleasing to evoke the rocky expanses and dunes, with a touch of the presence of the plant world.

LAKE TITICACA

CACTUS

The shores around Lake Titicaca are green and wet, but beyond them are arid places with magnificent varieties of cactus and succulents. If there is sufficient light, the plants will flower when good weather arrives.

CARE

Difficulty	♣ ♣ ♧
Water	● ● ◗
Light	☀ ☀ ☀
Container	🗋 📗 🗋 ❘ 🗒

SUPPLIES

Glass jar (about 7½ in/19 cm diameter, 7½ in/19 cm high), without lid
Measuring cup
Plant mister or fresh sponge
Pencil
Rose pruning gloves or a sheet of paper

LIFETIME

These plants cannot be pruned. After several years, they may have to be moved to a larger container.

INGREDIENTS

2 *Pilosocereus azureus* (bluetorch cactus)
1 *Rebutia*
2½ cups/600 ml red volcanic stone*
1¾ cups/400 ml planting mix (⅞ cup/200 ml of each potting soil for indoor plants and sand)*
2 handfuls of fine gravel, gray*
3 handfuls of fine gravel, black*
5 handfuls of medium gravel, white*
2 granite pebbles*
2 pieces of driftwood*
⅓ cup/75 ml filtered water

*See the list of materials on pages 61–79.

STEP-BY-STEP

1. Carefully clean the interior and exterior of the jar. Soak the base of the plants in filtered water for 5 minutes so that the root ball is well moistened.

2. Gently pour an even layer of the red volcanic stone into the bottom of the jar. Be careful not to damage the glass.

3. Pour the fine gray and black gravels and a handful of the white gravel in layers around the inside edge of the jar. Pour the planting mix evenly over the volcanic stones and gravels, making a bed about 1¼ in/3 cm deep.

4. Make three small wells in the soil where you want to put the plants, deep enough for the roots.

5. To unpot the cacti, push on the root ball with a pencil to avoid the spines.

6. Take hold of each cactus with the gloves or by rolling the cactus in paper (to avoid the spines), then gently loosen the roots. Place the plants in the wells and fill in the soil, pressing the plants in gently, and then tamp down the soil around them.

7. Water the soil evenly at the foot of the plants with filtered water, using a plant mister (or soak a sponge and gently squeeze it over the soil).

8. Lay the rest of the white and black gravel on the soil. Add the pebbles and the driftwood.

9. Place the terrarium in a bright place out of direct sunlight. Take care of the terrarium following the advice on pages 20–27 (dry terrarium).

MACHU PICCHU
SUCCULENTS

A sacred abandoned city in the Andes, Machu Picchu is built of brown and
gray local stone, enriched with vegetation in intense, varied shades of green.
This is the inspiration for the elements in this beautiful dry terrarium.

CARE

Difficulty
Water
Light
Container

SUPPLIES

Glass jar (about 10¼ in/26 cm
diameter, 10¼ in/26 cm high),
without lid
Measuring cup
Plant mister or fresh sponge

VARIATION

This type of design can be done
with most types of succulents or
cactus, as long as their size allows.

INGREDIENTS

2 *Portulacaria afra*
1 *Aeonium arborium*
1 *Sedum burrito*
1 *Euphorbia ingens*
3½ cups/800 ml red volcanic stone*
2½ cups/600 ml planting mix (1¼ cups/300 ml of
each potting soil for indoor plants and sand)*
3 handfuls of fine gravel, black*
2 handfuls of medium gravel, gray*
10 handfuls of coarse crushed gravel, gray and
white*
2 big granite pebbles*
5 pieces of driftwood*
⅝ cup/150 ml filtered water

*See the list of materials on pages 61–79.

STEP-BY-STEP

1 . Carefully clean the interior and exterior of the jar. Soak the base of the plants in filtered water for 5 minutes so that the root ball is well moistened.

2 . Gently pour an even layer of the red volcanic stone into the bottom of the jar. Be careful not to damage the glass.

3 . Pour the black and gray gravel and two handfuls of the coarse crushed gravel in layers around the inside edge of the jar.

4 . Pour the planting mix evenly over the volcanic stones and gravels, making a bed about 1½ in/4 cm deep.

5 . Make four small wells in the soil deep enough for the roots of the plants.

6 . Gently loosen the roots. Place the plants in the wells and fill in the soil, pressing the plants in gently, and then tamp down the soil around them.

7 . Water the soil evenly at the foot of the plants with filtered water, using a plant mister (or soak a sponge and gently squeeze it over the soil). Be careful not to get the base of the leaves wet, which could cause the plants to rot.

8 . Lay the rest of the coarse gray and white gravel on the soil, covering it entirely.

9 . Add the granite pebbles and the driftwood.

10 . Place the terrarium in a bright place out of direct sunlight. Take care of the terrarium following the advice on pages 20–27 (dry terrarium).

POPOCATÉPETL

SEDUM

This design brings together plants from a semiarid environment,
like the habitat around the volcano Popocatépetl in Mexico.

CARE

Difficulty	◆	◇	◇
Water	●	●	●
Light	☀	☀	☀
Container	▯	▮	▯	◖

SUPPLIES

Hanging glass globe (about
  8 in/20 cm diameter)
Measuring cup
Plant mister or fresh sponge
Small scissors

EASY PLANTS

Sedums are well adapted to
terrariums. They resist the cold but
absolutely need a well-drained
substrate to thrive.

INGREDIENTS

3 different *Sedums*
2¼ cups/500 ml red volcanic stone*
1¾ cups/400 ml planting mix (⅞ cups/200 ml
  of each potting soil for indoor plants and
  river sand)*
3 handfuls of fine gravel, black*
3 handfuls of medium gravel, white*
2 handfuls of coarse crushed gravel, gray*
2 granite pebbles*
⅝ cup/150 ml filtered water

*See the list of materials on pages 61–79.

194

1 . Carefully clean the interior and exterior of the jar. Soak the base of the plants in filtered water for 5 minutes so that the root ball is well moistened.

2 . Gently pour an even layer of the red volcanic stone into the bottom of the globe. Be careful not to damage the glass.

3 . Pour half the black and white gravels in layers around the inside edge of the jar.

4 . Pour the planting mix evenly over the volcanic stones and gravels, making a bed about 1¼ in/3 cm deep.

5. Make small wells in the soil deep enough for the roots of the plants. Gently loosen the roots. Place the plants in the wells and fill in the soil, pressing the plants in gently, and then tamp down the soil around them.

6. Water the soil evenly at the foot of the plants with filtered water, using a plant mister (or soak a sponge and gently squeeze it over the soil). Be careful not to get the plants themselves wet.

7. Lay the rest of the white and black gravel at the base of the plants and on the soil surface. Add the crushed gray gravel and arrange the granite pebbles.

8. Take care of the terrarium following the advice on pages 20–27 (dry terrarium).

SOUTH AFRICA
NATAL
SUCCULENTS

On the steppes of Kwazulu-Natal, vegetation is composed mostly of small, dense bushes that are succulents, known for their capacity to retain water and to limit their needs, as in this design.

CARE
Difficulty
Water
Light
Container

SUPPLIES
Glass jar (about 8¾ in/22 cm diameter, 13½ in/34 cm high), without lid
Measuring cup
Plant mister or fresh sponge
Small scissors

DISCREET PLANTS
Three or four plants can be grown in this limited space: succulents of this type are well adapted to thrive in a small space without competing.

INGREDIENTS
1 *Crassula pseudolycopodioides* (pot diameter 2½ in/6 cm)
1 *Crassula pyramidalis* (pot diameter 2½ in/6 cm)
1 *Euphorbia pugniformis* (pot diameter 2½ in/6 cm)
1⅔ cups/400 ml red volcanic stone*
2 cups/450 ml planting mix (⅓ cups/300 ml potting soil for indoor plants, ⅔ cup/150 ml sand)*
2 handfuls of fine gravel, light gray and white*
1 handful of coarse gravel, beige*
2 granite pebbles*
⅓ cup/75 ml filtered water

*See the list of materials on pages 61–79.

STEP-BY-STEP

1 . Carefully clean the interior and exterior of the jar. Soak the base of the plants in filtered water for 5 minutes so that the root ball is well moistened.

2 . Gently pour an even layer of the red volcanic stone into the bottom of the jar. Be careful not to damage the glass.

3 . Pour half the fine gravels in layers around the inside edge of the jar.

4 . Pour the planting mix evenly over the volcanic stones and gravels. Make three wells in the soil deep enough for the roots of the plants. Gently loosen the roots. Place the plants in the wells and fill in the soil, pressing the plants in gently, and then tamp down the soil around them.

5 . Water the soil evenly at the foot of the plants with filtered water, using a plant mister (or soak a sponge and gently squeeze it over the soil). Be careful not to get the plants' upper parts wet.

6 . Lay the rest of the fine gravel and the coarse beige gravel at the foot of the plants. Set the granite pebbles on the fine gravels. Take care of the terrarium following the advice on pages 20–27 (dry terrarium).

KRUGER NATIONAL PARK

PORTULACARIA AND HAWORTHIA

Many semiarid plant species are native to this great reserve in South Africa.
With this design, we hope to evoke a landscape rich in robust plants.

CARE

Difficulty
Water
Light
Container

SUPPLIES

Glass jar (about 12 in/30 cm
  diameter, 20 in/50 cm high),
  without lid
Measuring cup
Plant mister or fresh sponge
Small scissors

DID YOU KNOW?

Native to southern Africa,
Portulacaria afra is a dense shrub
with thick foliage. It is favored by
herbivores, especially elephants,
who can consume 350 lbs/160 kg
each day.

INGREDIENTS

1 *Portulacaria afra*, here, a 5-year-old bonsai (pot
  diameter about 6 in/15 cm)
1 *Haworthia fasciata* (pot diameter 2½ in/6 cm)
4½ cups/1 L red volcanic stone*
3¾ cups/900 ml planting mix (2 cups/450 ml of
  each potting soil for indoor plants, river sand, and
  fine sand)*
4 handfuls of fine gravel, black*
2 handfuls of fine gravel, gray*
2 handfuls of fine gravel, white*
2 handfuls of small black pebbles*
2 handfuls of river sand*
3 granite pebbles*
⅝ cup/150 ml filtered water

*See the list of materials on pages 61–79.

STEP-BY-STEP

1. Carefully clean the interior and exterior of the jar. Soak the base of the plants in filtered water for 5 minutes so that the root ball is well moistened.

2. Gently pour an even layer of the red volcanic stone into the bottom of the jar. Be careful not to damage the glass.

3. Pour half the fine black gravel in a layer around the inside edge of the jar. Make two more layers with the gray and white gravels.

4. Pour the planting mix evenly over the volcanic stones and gravel, making a bed about 3/8 in/1 cm deep.

5 . Make two small wells in the soil deep enough for the roots of the plants. Gently loosen the roots. Place the plants in the wells and fill in the soil, pressing the plants in gently, and then tamp down the soil around them.

6 . Water the soil evenly at the foot of the plants with filtered water, using a plant mister (or soak a sponge and gently squeeze it over the soil). Be careful not to get water on the leaves of the haworthia.

7 . Arrange the river sand and the rest of the fine black gravel at the foot of the plants in layers and add the small black pebbles, so as to cover all the soil and thus hold moisture in the ground. Arrange the granite pebbles.

8 . Take care of the terrarium following the advice on pages 20–27 (dry terrarium).

GALILEE

OLIVE, THYME

Thyme and olive get along well together where they grow naturally around the Mediterranean. This landscape evokes beautiful scenes of peaceful times, with the sweet scent of thyme.

CARE

Difficulty	🌿	🌿	🌿
Water	💧	💧	💧
Light	☀	☀	☀
Container	⬜	⬜	⬛	▱

SUPPLIES

Glass jar (about 11 in/28 cm diameter, 20 in/50 cm high), without lid
Measuring cup
Plant mister or fresh sponge
Small scissors

GROW AN OLIVE TREE

It is not easy to find a small olive tree, so we chose a large container. For a smaller design, you can try to germinate an olive pit.

INGREDIENTS

1 olive tree, here, a 5-year-old bonsai (pot diameter 6 in/15 cm)
1 thyme plant (pot diameter 3 in/7.5 cm)
4½ cups/1 L red volcanic stone*
6¼ cups/1.5 L planting mix (2½ cups/600 ml potting soil for indoor plants, 2½ cups/600 ml clay, 1¼ cups/300 ml river sand)*
2 handfuls of fine gravel, light gray*
1 handful of fine gravel, white*
2 handfuls of slate chips*
1 handful of fine river sand*
⅝ cup/150 ml filtered water

*See the list of materials on pages 61–79.

STEP-BY-STEP

1. Carefully clean the interior and exterior of the jar. Soak the base of the plants in filtered water for 5 minutes so that the root ball is well moistened.

2. Gently pour an even layer of the red volcanic stone into the bottom of the jar. Be careful not to damage the glass.

3. Pour half the fine gray gravel and all the white gravel in layers around the inside edge of the jar.

4. Pour the planting mix evenly over the volcanic stones and gravels, making a bed about 2¾ in/7 cm deep.

5 . Make two small wells in the soil deep enough for the roots of the olive and thyme. Gently loosen the roots. Place the plants in the wells and fill in the soil, pressing the plants in gently, and then tamp down the soil around them.

6 . Water the soil evenly at the foot of the plants with filtered water, using a plant mister (or soak a sponge and gently squeeze it over the soil).

7 . Arrange the river sand and the rest of the fine gray gravel at the foot of the plants in layers, and the slate chips around the rest of the soil so it is all covered. Take care of the terrarium following the advice on pages 20–27 (dry terrarium).

MONTE CINTO

MYRTLE

Myrtus communis, or myrtle is a characteristic shrub of the Corsican landscape. It is one of the emblematic plants of the Corsican *maquis*, which we evoke with this design.

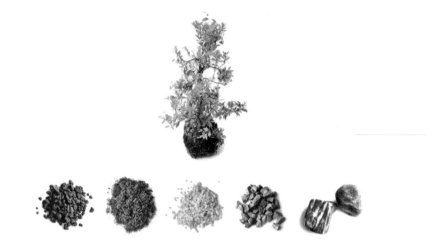

CARE

Difficulty	🌿	🌿	◻
Water	💧	◌	◌
Light	☀	☀	☀
Container	◻	◻	◼	◻

SUPPLIES

Glass jar (about 11 in/28 cm
  diameter, 20 in/50 cm high),
  with lid
Measuring cup
Plant mister or fresh sponge
Small scissors

A LONG HISTORY

The Bible has many references to
myrtle. In Greco-Roman mythology,
it is one of the symbols of Venus
and Jupiter.

INGREDIENTS

1 *Myrtus communis* bonsai (here, 5 years old)
3½ cups/800 ml red volcanic stone*
4¼ cups/1 L planting mix (3 cups/700 ml regular
  potting soil, 1¼ cups/300 ml river sand)*
3 handfuls of fine gravel, light gray*
4 handfuls of crushed gravel, gray*
3 large granite pebbles
⅞ cup/200 ml filtered water

*See the list of materials on pages 61–79.

1 . Carefully clean the interior and exterior of the jar. Soak the base of the myrtle in filtered water for 5 minutes so that the root ball is well moistened.

2 . Gently pour an even layer of the red volcanic stone into the bottom of the jar. Be careful not to damage the glass. You can keep some to decorate the surface.

3 . Arrange half the fine gravel in a layer around the inside edge of the jar.

4 . Pour the planting mix evenly over the volcanic stones and gravel, making a bed about 2½ in/6 cm deep.

5 . Make a well in the soil, in the center, deep enough for the roots. Gently loosen the roots. Place the myrtle in the well and fill in the soil, pressing it in gently, and then tamp down the soil around it.

6 . Water the soil evenly at the foot of the plant with filtered water, using a plant mister (or soak a sponge and gently squeeze it over the soil).

7 . Arrange the rest of the fine gravel at the foot of the myrtle; include the red volcanic stone if you kept some. Add the gray crushed gravel to cover the soil evenly. Set the granite pebbles in the crushed gravel.

8 . Close the jar after 72 hours. Take care of the terrarium following the advice on pages 20–27 (wet terrarium).

THE AFRICAN GREAT LAKES
LAKE TANGANYIKA
AQUATIC PLANTS

The secret heart of an arid desert is an oasis teeming with water and life. This design attempts to recreate the delicacy of an environment of water plants, such as what can be found in lakes and rivers around the world.

CARE

Difficulty	🍂 🍂 🍂
Water	💧 💧 💧
Light	☀ ☀ ☀
Container	🫙 🫙 🫙 ∣ 🪣

SUPPLIES

Glass jar (about 12 in/30 cm diameter, 20 in/50 cm high), without lid
Measuring cup
Aquarium pump and hose
Wire screen, fine
Lamp and grow light (6,400 K)
Clippers

TERRARIUM OR AQUARIUM?

Your aquatic garden can be inhabited by fish (pictured here, guppies). Ask the advice of an aquarium expert.

INGREDIENTS

1 *Eichhornia crassipes* (water hyacinth)
1 *Cabomba caroliniana*
1 *Alternanthera philoxeroides*
6½ cups/1.5 L red volcanic stone*
5 handfuls of fine gravel, gray*
3 handfuls of medium gravel, white*
5 handfuls of crushed gravel, gray*
5 gray granite pebbles*
Enough filtered water to fill the container to three-quarters full

*See the list of materials on pages 61–79.

If water hyacinth is considered invasive where you live, substitute *Nymphaea* (King of Siam water lily).
If *Cabomba* is considered invasive where you live, substitute *Ceratophyllum demersum* (hornwort).
If *Alternanthera* is considered invasive where you live, substitute *Micromeria brownei* (creeping charlie).

Caution. A design of this size filled with water can weigh more than 65 lbs/30 kg and be very unwieldy to move. Please take this into account and also be careful about the strength and water-tightness of the container chosen, especially if in proximity to electrical equipment.

1 . Carefully clean the interior and exterior of the jar. Rinse the volcanic stones and the gravels repeatedly in clear water. Place the pump in the bottom of the container. The pump ensures water circulation, preventing it from stagnating. Connect the hose.

2 . Place the screen over the pump, cutting a hole for the hose to pass through. The screen keeps the gravel from obstructing the water intake in the pump.

3 . Carefully spread the red volcanic stone on the bottom of the container, allowing the hose to stand up. Use the crushed gravel to hold the pump in position.

4 . Arrange the *Cabomba* and the *Alternanthera* on the bottom, covering their feet with gravel. Add the granite pebbles.

5. Carefully pour water down the wall of the container to avoid disturbing the gravel at the bottom or damaging the plants. When the water level reaches 8 in/20 cm from the top, make sure that the end of the hose is well out of the water. Place the water hyacinth on the surface and let it float.

6. Connect the power to the pump and check that the water is flowing from the hose nozzle.

7. To avoid water stagnation, use a 6,400 K lamp next to the water garden. It is also advised to change one quarter of the volume of water every month.

GLOSSARY

BIOTOPE
A location where physical and chemical conditions permit the development of a certain ecosystem. This environment hosts a group of living organisms (fauna, flora, fungi, microorganisms).

BONSAI
The art of bonsai involves cultivation of a tree while suppressing its growth, to create a miniature tree. Using techniques of pruning roots and binding stems and branches, the plant is given the contorted forms of a tree on a reduced scale. Nearly all tree species can be transformed into bonsai.

DECIDUOUS
Foliage is not perennial: it falls in winter and regrows in the spring.

ECOSYSTEM
A system characterized by the interaction of its different elements (animals, plants, minerals) within a given natural environment, forming a perennial biological cycle.

EVERGREEN
Foliage is not subject to the seasons: leaves remain on the tree throughout the year.

PERENNIAL
Temperate zone plant of which a part (bulb, roots) survives the winter to fully regrow each spring.

SUBSTRATE
The soil in which a plant sets its roots and finds its nutrients.

SUCCULENT
Succulents are also sometimes called "fat plants." Their name comes from the Latin *succulentus*, meaning "full of juice," evoking the thick, fleshy character of these plants. This physical trait permits them to store maximum water and nutrients so as to provide themselves with water over long periods; succulents easily survive this way in arid habitats.

SOURCES

GREEN FACTORY

Anna and Noam invite you to their atelier-boutique in Paris and offer you finished terrariums, kits to create terrariums, and all the materials that you will need for your designs (mosses, pebbles, planting mix, plants . . .).

17, rue Lucien Sampaix
Paris 10
www.greenfactory.fr

While your local home, garden, and design stores are great places to start looking for terrarium supplies, here are a few online spots you might find helpful.

FOR CONTAINERS
Anchor Hocking – www.anchorhocking.com
Ikea – www.ikea.com
Save-on-crafts – www.save-on-crafts.com
Sprout Home – www.sprouthome.com
Terrain – www.shopterrain.com
West Elm – www.westelm.com

FOR PLANTS
Arizona Aquatic Gardens – www.azgardens.com
Aquarium Plants – www.aquariumplants.com
Forest Farm at Pacifica – www.forestfarm.com
Moss Acres – www.mossacres.com
Simply Succulents – www.simplysucculents.com
Sprout Home – www.sprouthome.com
The Air Plant Shop – www.airplantshop.com

VISUAL INDEX OF TERRARIUM DESIGNS

TROPICAL LANDSCAPES

Taman Negara **82**

Khao Yai **86**

Kunming **90**

Yuelu **94**

Anhui **98**

Sigiriya **102**

Angkor Wat **106**

Ta Prohm **110**

Amazonian Park **114**

Tikal **118**

Orinoco **122**

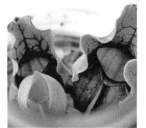

Roraima **126**

Chiapas **130**

Sierra Gorda **134**

Gorongosa **138**

TEMPERATE LANDSCAPES

Fontainebleau **144**

Chambord **148**

Ashdown Forest **152**

Val di Cornia **156**

The Black Forest **160**

Kahurangi **164**

Oshima Island **168**

Kyushu **172**

Mount Luofu **176**

Lake Tai **180**

ARID LANDSCAPES

Lake Titicaca **186**

Machu Picchu **190**

Popocatépetl **194**

Natal **198**

Kruger National Park **202**

Galilee **206**

Monte Cinto **210**

Lake Tanganyika **214**

INDEX

First published in the United States of America in 2018 by Chronicle Books LLC.
Originally published in France in 2016 under the title *Terrariums: Les Mondes Végétaux Sous Verre* by Marabout.

Library of Congress Cataloging-in-Publication Data available.
ISBN 978-1-4521-7009-1

Manufactured in China

Photographs by Rebecca Genet
Cover design by Vanessa Dina

10 9 8 7 6 5 4 3 2 1

Chronicle books and gifts are available at special quantity discounts to corporations, professional associations, literacy programs, and other organizations. For details and discount information, please contact our corporate/premiums department at corporatesales@chroniclebooks.com or at 1-800-759-0190.

Chronicle Books LLC
680 Second Street
San Francisco, California 94107
www.chroniclebooks.com